Antique American Country Furniture

Antique American Country Furniture

A FIELD GUIDE

by Thomas M. Voss

ILLUSTRATED BY DONALD BENDER

J. B. Lippincott Company · Philadelphia and New York

749.213
V
c.1

The epigraph from John T. Kirk,
The Impecunious Collector's Guide to American Antiques,
copyright 1975, is reprinted by permission
of Alfred A. Knopf, Inc.

U.S. Library of Congress Cataloging in Publication Data

Voss, Thomas M   birth date
  Antique American country furniture.

  Bibliography: p.
  Includes indexes.
  1. Country furniture—United States—Handbooks,
manuals, etc.   I. Title.
NK2405.V67   749.2′13   77-15898
ISBN-0-397-01219-5
ISBN-0-397-01267-5 (Pbk.)

For old friends—
you know who you are—
and for everyone who understands
"the delicate exactness of pure chance"

CONTENTS

ACKNOWLEDGMENTS

For their generosity in sharing with me both materials and knowledge and their constant encouragement in the writing of this book I express my special thanks to four extraordinary denizens of the antiques world: Robert Lutz, Samuel Pennington, Charles Santore, and Lita Solis-Cohen. Without them this book might never have been written, and certainly its content would have suffered.

I also gratefully acknowledge the help and encouragement of Elsie Byers, Joseph Franklin, Walt Laughlin, and Val Tyler.

"Out there somewhere is
the finest of its kind at a bargain price.
You all have a chance, and if you don't get it,
the ghost of Ezra Peters will!"

—CHRIS HUNTINGTON,
quoted in *Maine Antique Digest*

"It is necessary to be a Sherlock Holmes
of furniture."

—JOHN T. KIRK,
*The Impecunious Collector's Guide
to American Antiques*

IN BRIEF:
HOW TO USE
THIS BOOK

This field guide to antique American country furniture can be used in several different ways depending on what sort of information you are after.

1. For general information on country furniture—buying, construction, authenticating, dating, characteristics of the periods and styles of furniture, prices—see Chapters 1 through 5;

2. For specific information on the various forms of country furniture—construction, authenticating, illustrations, names, chronology, dating, provenance, availability, prices—see Chapters 6 through 13;

3. For definitions of terms used in this book and by antiques collectors, dealers, and auctioneers, plus a name index for the pieces in Chapters 6 through 13, see the Glossary;

4. For quick comparison of a piece that you see in person with a piece illustrated in Chapters 6 through 13, see the Picture Index;

5. For quick style classification of the pieces illustrated in Chapters 6 through 13, see the Style Index.

For more detailed information on how to use this book, please read the Introduction.

INTRODUCTION

This is a book to be taken with you whenever and wherever you go stalking antique American country furniture in the field—whether antiques shops, auctions, flea markets, dusty attics, or damp barns. It is the kind of book that I myself would have wanted when I first started collecting because it not only illustrates and describes the basic types and styles of country antiques but also includes information on dating, construction, fakery, availability, and much more. It is above all intended to be a practical but readable book, filled with important information in condensed form, ready for instant reference at all times. And unlike many antiques books, it does not have illustrations of pieces that are now peacefully dozing in museums. Rather, 99 percent of the pieces illustrated here have recently been sold on the open market. Many of them are of "museum quality," but they are now being appreciated and used in the homes of happy collectors.

If you are unfamiliar with antique country furniture but want to know more, this book will provide something of a crash course on the subject. If you are a more experienced collector, I hope that you will find here the information you need to help you avoid the costly mistakes we are all prone to make when we are tempted to buy a piece whose authenticity or age we are uncertain of.

While organizing this book for clarity, usefulness, and compactness, I made certain assumptions that I feel you should be aware of. First, I have assumed that, although you may know next to nothing about antique American country furniture, you have a strong desire to learn as much about it as you can in the shortest possible time. This does not mean that you must be a country furniture "nut," as I am. Rather, it means I hope you think that collecting antiques may be fun but also realize that to do it well requires an investment of some time and effort; that, for whatever reasons, you believe that early handmade objects are often more desirable than machine-made objects but are willing to admit that just because something is old does not necessarily make it good; that you have a desire for accurate, truthful information about country furniture, in part because you do not like being cheated in any area where you spend your hard-earned dollars; and that you have an open enough mind to shed any preconceived notions you may have about antiques if you are offered what may be better ideas.

Second, I hope you keep in mind that this book is a field guide. As such, I have written it with the assumption that you will be using it, in part, while comparing actual objects "in the field" with information about those objects in this book. You will, I feel, realize the full benefits of this book only if you take it along when you go antiquing.

I have not tried in this book to illustrate exhaustively every piece of country furniture that exists—an impossible, pointless task precluded by the sheer design diversity of country furniture (which is also one of its delights). Even dealers who have been in business for more than a quarter of a century and have handled thousands of pieces will tell you that on any given day they may turn up a piece that holds fascinating surprises for them. Instead, I have taken an approach that will allow you to "zero in" on almost any aspect of any form of country furniture and of almost every variation of that form.

In Chapters 1 through 5 you will find general information about antique American country furniture. Here are tips on where and how to buy it, information on how it is made and what to look for when authenticating and dating it, and what I feel is a clear explanation of the styles and periods of American furniture and their importance to you. This is basic knowledge that will become second nature to you as your firsthand experience with antiques increases.

Chapters 6 through 13 narrow all this down to specific information about the forms of country furniture. Each chapter deals with a specific form, such as the chair, the table, or the desk. At the beginning of each chapter is a "map" of the form pointing out the names of most of its parts. This will help you to understand the notes that follow on the construction of the form. Next comes an examination checklist that tells you what to look for in the way of restorations and fakery in the individual form. Finally, there are illustrations and descriptions of the form's variations, including information on names, dates, origins, availability, price, and, when necessary, further notes on construction.

You will notice that for each piece or group of pieces illustrated at least *two* sets of dates are given. The first, in parentheses following the name of the variation, tells you the entire time span during which that variation was made, and these time spans are themselves arranged in chronological order within each chapter. This method of dating will immediately tell you the earliest and latest dates when a particular form's variation was made in America and should also give you some sense of the form's historical development. Thus, for example, if you look in Chapter 11, Desks (the form), under figs. 111–13, the Slant-Lid Desk (a variation of the form), you will see that this type of desk was made from as early as about 1700 through as late as 1840; however, another desk variation, the Tambour Desk, fig. 117, was made from only about 1790 through 1840. Now you know that the slant-lid desk developed before the tambour desk; and you also know that if you found a tambour desk in an antiques shop that was dated 1760, something would be amiss.

The second set of dates given in the text is for the individual piece illustrated. The stylistic features and other aspects of a piece allow us to place it within a certain range of years. (This concept of dating by stylistic features will become much clearer to you after you have read Chapter 4, Periods and Styles of American Furniture.) Although the illustrations have usually been selected to represent commonly found pieces, you may very well find one that does not look exactly like one that is pictured. What do you do then?

First, you would identify the variation of the form. In the case of desks, you would ask yourself, "What kind of desk is this—a slant-lid desk, a desk on frame, a tambour desk, a fall-front desk, etc.?" Next, you would locate one or more other pieces in this book with similar design features, and you would use the dates for those pieces as the basis for dating the piece you are examining (assuming that the piece is a genuine antique). Remember, too, that just because you are looking at a desk does not mean that other desks are the only pieces in this book to refer to when dating it. For example, a desk on frame is really nothing more than a desk set on a tablelike base; therefore, one of the tables illustrated in Chapter 9 may have exactly the design features you are looking for.

The Glossary is somewhat different from those in other antiques books. First, it contains not only definitions of terms used in this book and by antiques collectors, dealers, and auctioneers in describing the construction methods and stylistic features of country furniture but also some of the specialized jargon used in the antiques world. Through cross-references, the Glossary will guide you to appropriate illustrations in the book for clarification, when necessary. Second, the Glossary contains the name and figure number of every piece illustrated in Chapters 6 through 13 and so also serves as a name index for the book.

Following the Glossary is the Picture Index, which shows in reduced size every illustration in Chapters 6 through 13, along with its figure number. This will help you to locate quickly any piece in the book and may also be used in conjunction with the cross-references in the Glossary.

Finally, there is the Style Index, which lists under its main heads the names of the various styles of American furniture and under its subheads the form and figure number of every piece in Chapters 6 through 13 that can be categorized as being in that style (or combination of styles). The Style Index will help you understand how the design features of a piece relate to dating it. Furthermore, it will give you an instant reference when reading auction or other advertisements. For example, if an auction advertisement lists a "Chippendale chest of drawers," you could immediately locate any illustrations of such pieces in this book first by looking under the main head, Chippendale, and then under the subhead, Chests of Drawers.

Antique American country furniture—appreciating, living with, and using it—is one of the great pleasures of my life, and I hope that this book will contribute to making it one of yours, too.

Part I

WHAT IS ANTIQUE COUNTRY FURNITURE?
1

There is some controversy among experts over what we should call country furniture, and even whether we should always use the term "country." Some like to distinguish among homemade, primitive, rustic, and country furniture. But we can machete our way through this small jungle of entangled terminology because "country" is the term most widely used, understood, and preferred among collectors and dealers.

Some, including the United States Customs, say that an antique is simply an object that is more than one hundred years old. That definition would, of course, include Victorian objects. For our purposes, the significant criteria for country furniture are that it was made by hand away from an urban center in America before 1840.

As usual, there are exceptions that we have to live with.

First, some pieces that many country furniture collectors consider very desirable were made after 1840. Shaker furniture is a good example, but there are others. I use the date 1840 because factory mass production of furniture was then becoming widespread. Factories even began to imitate handmade country forms in order to sell their products in rural areas. Yet, in dwindling numbers, country craftsmen continued to make furniture by hand, since industrialization came later to the country than to the city. Taking this into account, you may assume that any piece in this book that is dated as late as 1840 may also have been made after that date.

Another exception is that certain urban craftsmen who made elegant, high-style furniture also made furniture for the country trade. William Savery of Philadelphia is a good example of this. But since the pieces attributed to him for rural consumption are in the country taste—albeit high-style country taste— we can still consider them country furniture. Also, some craftsmen such as Eliphalet Chapin of East Windsor, Connecticut, learned their trade in the city—Philadelphia, in his case— and then returned to the country to work and to sell their products. Chapin's pieces could also be called high-style country, but they meet our criteria above.

Perhaps the most glaring exceptions are the famous Hitchcock chairs, which were made in the country but in furniture factories. Are they country antiques? All I can say is that if you like that sort of furniture and think of it as antique—as opposed to semiantique—more power to you. Examples of Hitchcock furniture are represented in this book.

Although country furniture was made in the seventeenth century, most of what we see and buy today dates from the eighteenth and nineteenth centuries, when expansion into rural areas began in earnest. Thus, it is difficult to label as country furniture such extremely rare seventeenth-century forms as wainscot chairs, court cupboards, and Hadley chests. They were, and are, furniture for the wealthy, although if you found such a piece at a price less than that of a Rolls Royce Camargue, you might consider purchasing it. For these reasons, I have not included such pieces in this book.

Country furniture frequently reflects the design features of high-style period furniture—Queen Anne, Chippendale, Hepplewhite, and the like. But usually the country craftsman created his furniture from his memory of period pieces rather than from actual models or from furniture style books. The result is that his solutions to design problems may be unique and in many cases more inventive than those of the high-style furniture on which he may have based his own work. In other words, country furniture often has a more distinctly American look than high-style furniture.

The more you appreciate country furniture, the more it will be clear to you that *country* does not mean *crude*. For some reason, many people have an image of our predecessors as living in log cabins with the most simple of furniture. It is true that some country pieces seem to have been slapped together haphazardly, but those pieces were often meant to be "disposable"—used only until better furniture could be made or afforded. Many country pieces were made with the same careful attention to design and sound construction principles that were used in creating their city cousins. The fittest of these pieces have survived because they were better made, better loved, and, therefore, better cared for by their owners over the years.

Finally, remember that some pieces straddle the fence between the country and the city. The Windsor chair is a good example. Even a fine Philadelphia comb-back Windsor chair, as in fig. 28, would be equally at home in a country or urban setting, which could never be said of a fine Philadelphia Chippendale chair.

WHERE AND HOW
TO BUY
COUNTRY ANTIQUES
2

Antiques can be found at dealers' shops, antiques shows, auctions, flea markets, garage sales, tag sales, your Aunt Harriet's attic—even on the front porches of strangers. In other words, antiques are where you find them, and each place you find them requires different buying techniques.

To my mind, part of the fun of collecting antiques is buying them at bargain prices, below market value. Here's an example of what I mean. Early one morning at a local flea market a flea marketeer was selling a chair for $75 that he had recently purchased from a private party for $5. Without any haggling, he quickly sold the chair to an antiques dealer. That dealer is now asking $1,000 for the chair. He must have been ecstatic to have found it at such a bargain price, since it was a Carver chair, a rare type made about 1700. Obviously, it takes luck to get a bargain like that, but, as you will see, there are ways of enhancing your luck.

In order to know whether or not you are getting a bargain, you must have a good idea of the current market value of the pieces that interest you. The best way to acquire this knowledge is to visit shows, dealers, and auctions and find out how much pieces are selling for and how much people are willing to pay for them. You can supplement these firsthand excursions into the real world with price books and periodicals that tell you what pieces actually sold for or what price is being asked for them. Also, auction catalogs sometimes list the prices the auction house believes the pieces it is selling will bring.

AUCTIONS

You can really enjoy yourself at a lively auction and maybe even get a bargain, but you can also lose your shirt as fast as you could in Las Vegas. Bidding and buying at auctions require good judgment, knowledge, and a cool head. Here are some pointers.

Be aware of whether the auction you plan to attend is "unreserved" or "reserved." In an unreserved auction, all pieces sell to the highest bidder—period. On the other hand, an auction in which one, several, or all of the pieces are reserved means that the owner, for whom the auctioneer is working, has set for each piece a minimum reserve price below which it will not be sold. If the highest bid does not reach this minimum, the piece is not sold but is "bought back" by the owner (who, by the way, may be the auctioneer himself).

One thing you must *never* do at an auction is buy anything that you have not first thoroughly inspected. A newspaper advertisement for one country auction I attended said that among the items for sale would be a "set of four chairs from Lancaster County, Pennsylvania." Lancaster County is one of those magic phrases that have the same effect on collectors of Pennsylvaniana as Pavlov's bell had on his dogs. Examining the chairs before the sale, I was disappointed to find that they were not antiques but only fairly good reproductions. The auctioneer never noted that fact when he sold them to the highest bidder for $1,200. Of course, the auctioneer never said they were antiques, either—that was for the buyer to know.

Many auctioneers are trustworthy folks whom you would not mind having over to your house for dinner. Others you would not let in the front door for fear they would make off with your best silver. Regardless of whether you think an auctioneer is honest or not, never trust him. If he has survived in business, it is primarily because he is a good salesman and earns his 20 percent commission. (One auctioneer I know started out as a door-to-door vacuum cleaner salesman and still gets ridiculously high prices for broken-down Eurekas.) Usually an auctioneer sells his goods "as is, where is." Unless he explicitly and unequivocally guarantees that what he is selling is an antique in a certain condition—and that he will take the piece back if it is not as advertised—do not believe what he says. Rely instead on your own knowledge, experience, and preauction inspection of the pieces that interest you. You can *always* inspect pieces before a sale, sometimes several days ahead of time. Do it.

Which brings us to bidding. After you have decided which pieces interest you, try to decide the top prices you will pay, as the best collectors always do. For when the bidding gets hot and heavy, and everyone seems to be fatally infected with that highly contagious disease called auction fever, your bankroll may quickly go up in smoke if you don't know when to stop bidding.

Here are a few bidding techniques you

might like to try. The first is to shut out a large part of the competition before the bidding can get too furious. The auctioneer usually begins the bidding at a price higher than what he thinks the opening bid will actually be. He will then ask for progressively lower and lower bids until someone jumps in. The lower the first bid, the more people will engage in bidding up the piece. Now, suppose you see a piece that you want, and your top price is $300. The auctioneer may ask for $200 to start, and no one will bid. By the time the opening bid is made, the price may have sunk to $50, at which point twenty people may jump on the bandwagon and bid the piece right up to $200 or more before you have had a chance to draw your next breath. This happens all the time, but perhaps if you had been smart enough to open the bidding at around $200, you might have shut out most of the competition. You might even have gotten the piece for your first and only bid. It has happened to me, although the auctioneer does not have to sell a piece on which only one bid has been made. And even if your strategy does not work and you lose the piece, at least you will have established your reputation at that auction as a tough competitor.

Another technique is jump bidding, which has been known to send other bidders into temporary shock. Suppose the bidding field has narrowed itself down to you and one or two other bidders, and you are afraid that soon the price will rise beyond your means. You can gain control of the bidding by making your next bid higher than the next acceptable bid. Suppose the price has reached $200 in twenty-dollar increments, the next acceptable bid being $220. Instead of bidding as usual with a wave of the hand or a nod of the head, loudly say "Two-fifty," or perhaps more if you can afford it. A jump bid or two will often knock out the competition because they may think that you are willing to pay almost any price.

Then there is the surprise bid, a very canny ploy. You lie low and do not enter the bidding at all, waiting for the moment when the auctioneer reaches a price level at which he is having a hard time coaxing a higher bid out of the audience. Wait a few seconds—let the high bidder think he has won—and then loudly jump bid. This can really disturb the other bidders because by this time they are keenly aware of their competition. When a higher bid is entered unexpectedly from left field, it can often steal the show as well as the piece being bid on.

The last technique—and perhaps the most common—is also the simplest to use. All you have to do is to conspicuously and immediately bid higher than your competitor each time he overbids you. One dealer I know simply keeps his hand up in the air, indicating that he is still bidding. This can be extremely unnerving for your opponent, as he begins to believe that no matter what he bids, you will up the ante.

A word of warning in all this: Although most auctioneers try to influence the bidding themselves by cajoling, telling jokes, or describing each piece in superlatives, a few auctioneers use much dirtier tricks. For example, an auctioneer may plant in the audience one or more shills, who make false bids. Or if he is a good actor, an auctioneer may take bids "out of the air," pretending that he has gotten a higher bid from somewhere when, in fact, he has not. An auctioneer will probably use such tricks early in the bidding because to use them later may leave him holding the bag, having himself bought what he was trying to sell. On the other hand, if the auctioneer does "buy" a piece, he may not mind; he may not have gotten the price he wanted, and he knows he can try to resell the piece at his next auction. Even if you suspect that such things are going on, you might as well stay at the auction if you are doing well. But if every piece is consistently bid out of your reach, call it a day.

As you attend more and more auctions, you

will begin to recognize dealers and collectors whom you have seen before and who may have "stolen" some pieces from you. You will learn what objects they usually buy and what prices they are willing to pay, and you will become familiar with their bidding styles, all of which should help you acquire what you want. Collectors usually have an advantage over dealers at an auction—they can often bid higher because they do not intend to make a profit on what they bought by reselling it immediately. On the other hand, a dealer may come to an auction to buy for a specific customer who may be willing to pay more than you can afford. Such is life.

Auctioneers aren't the only ones who use dirty tricks. Some dealers band together to form what is often called a "pool." Instead of bidding against each other—and perhaps driving the price of a piece beyond what they want to pay for it—the dealers agree that only one of them will bid on any given piece. When the regular auction is over, the pool members hold their own private mini-auction. The piece goes to the highest bidder, who is obligated to pay the auctioneer the high-bid price in the regular auction. The pool then splits up equally among themselves the difference between the high-bid price in the regular auction and the high-bid price in their mini-auction.

To clarify, suppose one dealer in a five-member pool bought a piece in the regular auction for $200, and in the pool's private mini-auction the piece went to another dealer for $300. The high bidder in the mini-auction would pay the regular auctioneer $200; he would then pay each member of the pool, including himself, one-fifth of the difference between $300 and $200, or $20. The high bidder's total investment is therefore $280, perhaps considerably less than he would have paid if all the dealers had been competing against each other. Also, each member of the pool will be $20 ahead, regardless of whether or not he bought anything.

But what effect, you might ask, can this possibly have on the bids of private collectors? Just this: The pool may pay too much for some things, too little for others, but *on the average* it pays less than the individual members would pay in unrestrained competition among themselves. Consequently, the pool has the ability to "hit" certain private bidders—to use its collective financial muscle to occasionally bid pieces beyond the reach of collectors. If the pool does this enough times, it has the effect of quickly silencing the bids of private collectors by making them feel that it is futile to bid against the pool.

Look around you at the next auction you attend. If you spot a group of people talking in muffled whispers, and one of them then steps forward to bid, you may be up against a pool. It may not make any difference, since the pool may not want the pieces you want or it may not be willing to bid as high as you are. In any case, it is important to be aware that the pool is operating because it may influence your bidding style, as discussed above.

Auction, or public sale, advertising can be found in antiques periodicals and in your local newspapers. Some auction galleries often hold catalog sales for which special illustrated booklets or fliers are published to advertise the sale. If you have to travel a great distance to inspect the sale items before the auction, having one of these catalogs may help you decide if it is worth it. Also, some of the catalogs of famous sales have themselves become collector's items!

ANTIQUES SHOPS

People go into business to make money, among other reasons, and so it is with antiques dealers. Some of them sell almost exclusively to other dealers, some buy and sell for museums and specific customers, and some largely deal with the public. One of the complaints I hear most often from dealers who sell to the public is that customers always think that by haggling they can buy a piece for a lower price than what is marked on it. Perhaps their complaints are justified. After all, would you haggle with a drugstore clerk over the price of a tube of toothpaste? On the other hand, many dealers *will* lower their prices if gently prodded in the right way. It doesn't always hurt to ask, "Is the price on this tavern table firm?"—especially after you have looked it over carefully, remarking on how much you admire it and, indirectly, the dealer's taste.

Another complaint I frequently hear, especially from dealers who have just attended an auction, is that they have almost identical pieces in their shops at lower prices than the pieces sold for at the auction, so why don't people buy from them instead of throwing their money away? This complaint is certainly justified, and it is a point to remember if you have the mistaken idea that dealers always sell at the highest possible retail prices. If that were true, dealers would not buy from each other.

Like auctioneers, dealers run the gamut from princes to cads. Many of them know what they are talking about most of the time and admit when they don't. Others pretend to be know-it-alls or else misrepresent the facts. In my experience, many dealers will tell you the truth about a piece as they know it, *but you must ask them.* Such questions as, "Is this American?", "When was it made?", "Where did you find it?", and "Are there any replaced or restored parts?" can get you a long way toward "psyching out" a dealer with whom you are unfamiliar—especially if you know the answers to most of the questions yourself! A dealer once told me that a dealer-friend of his is so anxious not to misrepresent what he sells that he "doesn't want to know too much" about what he has in stock. In any case, if you really examine a piece in a shop in detail—turning it over, looking at its back, front, and insides—a dealer will only respect you all the more. In fact, he may mistake you for another dealer.

There are as many kinds of shops selling country antiques as there are dealers, and each one will have the stamp of the dealer's personality. Among my favorite places to stalk antiques are shops that sometimes call themselves used furniture and antiques shops, and shops that specialize in objects other than country furniture, such as Victorian antiques shops. Used furniture and antiques shops—call them junk shops, if you want to—often have terrific stuff at rock-bottom prices, but you must be willing to burrow into and through piles of things that you don't want in order to find something that you do. And you must also be willing to get dirty in the process. Besides their low prices, what I like about junk shops is that they sell pieces in what is called "as found" condition; that is, the dealers don't refinish or alter what they sell. This greatly reduces the probabilities of buying a fake or an altered or improperly restored piece. Of course, it also increases the probability that you will have to have some restoration done on a piece, or, better still, do it yourself.

One more advantage: Victorian antiques shops—or Vicky shops as they are called in the trade—and others that do not specialize in country furniture often sell it at bargain prices because they want to get rid of it. Once I found a nice country Windsor chair for about half price in a shop that specializes in pre-Columbian antiquities! Searching through a Vicky shop may often be unproductive, but at least you probably won't feel like taking a bath afterward.

Of course, the easiest kind of shop in which to find country antiques is one that specializes in them. Even in a country antiques shop, you do not have to give up hunting for a "sleeper." After all, a dealer cannot be an expert in all areas and some things may be underpriced.

Unlike an auctioneer or a flea marketeer, a reputable country antiques dealer—that is, one who values his reputation and is interested in

doing business with you more than once—
should be ready and willing to guarantee in
writing that the piece he has sold you is what
he says it is. And he should exchange it or
refund your money if you later discover and
can prove that the piece is not as advertised.
This guarantee is nothing more than your receipt for your purchase, which must include a
written description listing the approximate
date of the piece, its condition with regard to
restorations or repairs, and even the name of
the maker, if known. Legally, your receipt is a
contract showing that you agreed to pay the
dealer a certain price for something of value
that he sold you. If he has misrepresented the
piece, and its value is not what he said it was, it
is a breach of contract and you can sue him if
you wish. Always ask for such a receipt-cum-
description when you are paying the market
price, or close to it, for a piece.

On the other hand, if you stumble across
your sleeper—and an old saw says there is one
in every shop—you may just want to buy it as
quickly as possible and be on your way with a
grin on your face. Once I came across a
Shaker bentwood rocker that I knew was
"right," but I would have been insane to ask
the dealer to guarantee it as such since it was
priced at about one-fifth of its market value.

He didn't know what it was, and I wasn't about to educate him.

There is a joke about two used car dealers, Mike and Joe, that goes like this. Mike had an old Chevy on his used car lot that Joe wanted to sell on his lot, so Joe bought it from Mike for $100. A few days later Mike decided that he had made a mistake, so he bought it back from Joe for $200. A week later Joe was sure he had a customer for the car, so he bought it back from Mike for $300. Well, this went on for a while until Joe finally did sell the car to a retail customer for $1,000. That same day Mike called Joe up and asked him if he could buy the car back again.

"Sorry," said Joe, "I sold it to a customer."

"Why did you have to do that?" said Mike. "We were making a good living off that car!"

Antiques dealers also sell to one another, and, as a result, prices escalate. You can learn a good deal about various dealers' markup policies and also their rationality by keeping tabs on the way prices rise as pieces change hands. Once I spotted an excellent bamboo-turned comb-back Windsor rocking chair in a shop window. They are supposed to be rare, but I did not want this one badly enough to pay $400 for it. All I could do was drool over it as the months passed and no one bought it.

Eventually it disappeared from the window. Then one day I went to an antiques show where a dealer I knew had a booth, and there was that same rocking chair. I took one look at the price and nearly went into cardiac arrest— $1,800! I do not visit that dealer's shop any longer, just on principle.

It is a good practice to become friendly with a few dealers and let them know that you are in the market for certain items. If they have your telephone number, you may get "first refusal rights" on many good things, especially if you have bought pieces from them in the past and they think of you as a good customer. And one related buying technique that you might like to try in order to secure a lower price works like this. You see a piece in a shop that you would really like to own, but the price is just too high. Rather than asking the dealer to reduce the price on the spot, you might say, in all truthfulness, "Well, I can't afford to pay $300, but if you ever decide to sell it for $250, perhaps you would give me a call. Here's my name and number." One of four things will happen: the dealer may scowl and refuse your name and number, in which case perhaps you should buy the piece at the asking price if you are really in love with it; he may reduce the price on the spot or try to reach a compromise; he may actually call you later; or he may sell the piece to someone else for his asking price. Whatever happens, you have little to lose by trying.

ANTIQUES SHOWS

Antiques shows are the shopping centers of the antiques world. Whether they are elegant and prestigious or just an annual event held at a local elementary school, they can offer you an unparalleled opportunity to educate yourself about antiques as well as to purchase good pieces for your collection.

You can find out what shows are scheduled for your area through advertisements in antiques periodicals, local newspapers, dealers, even roadside signs. Usually there will be an admission charge, and often the fees paid by dealers for booth space and by showgoers are collected for the benefit of some charitable organization, so you may be contributing to a good cause even if you do not buy anything. Local dealers may have cards in their shops announcing upcoming shows and offering a discount from the regular admission fee. Also, a good show may feature a lecture series by prominent experts or special exhibits of museum-quality objects.

What can you learn at an antiques show?

First, how much things cost. At a show, you can compare the prices of many dealers for similar pieces and thus get a good feel for the market. Also, dealers must pick and choose carefully what they bring to shows—obviously, they cannot transport their entire inventory unless it is very small. So you can also get an idea of what the dealers think is selling in the current market.

Shows also give you the opportunity to compare and evaluate hundreds, sometimes thousands, of pieces under one roof that months of traveling around the country might not afford. Of course, dealers do not display their wares so that the public can trek through their booths without buying anything. But they do not have much of a choice in the matter if you have come only to look. If you do decide to buy something, the same ground rules that apply to dealers in their shops apply to dealers at shows. But you should also plan to arrive at the show when the doors open, if possible; make a fast sweep through all the booths; return to any piece that caught your interest and examine it closely; and then *buy it.* At one show, I spotted a fine New England slat-back chair. Although it was reasonably priced, I left it, planning to return later to give it another look. Later, it turned out, was too late, because when I came back a woman was sitting in "my" chair, writing out a check for it. A dealer had beaten me to the punch.

Shows are usually restricted to dealers in genuine antiques, as opposed to "junque," and are often restricted to dealers in certain types of antiques. Local dealers should be able to tell you if a show will have enough country furniture to justify your attending it.

FLEA AND ANTIQUES MARKETS

If shows are the shopping centers of the antiques world, flea markets are the rummage sales. Most of them feature merchandise that is not worth writing home about for the collector of country furniture. On the other hand, flea markets offer perhaps the greatest opportunities for finding bargains, since the items sold there usually have not passed through very many dealers' hands before being offered for sale. Furthermore, the probabilities are higher that objects will not be recognized for what they are. For example, a pair of high-style Philadelphia Chippendale chairs in rough shape were recently offered for sale at a flea market in my area for $1,000 apiece. When no one bought them, they were put on the auction block at Sotheby Parke Bernet in New York, where the pair brought $27,000. I have gotten great, albeit less spectacular, bargains at flea markets, too. So can you.

Actually, there are two kinds of flea markets—general flea markets and antiques markets. At a general flea market you will find everything from houseplants to stretch socks to back issues of *National Geographic*. Squeezed in somewhere may be a dealer who is selling antiques, or maybe *one* antique. At antiques markets, as the name implies, many more of the dealers will be selling the genuine article.

Any buying dealer's cardinal rule about flea or antiques markets is *get there early*—find out when the market opens and be there. That's when the other buying dealers will be streaming in, and if you're just getting out of bed, you may as well stay there.

When a dealer arrives at a market to buy, he first scours the entire area looking for pieces that interest him. It's great exercise—by the time he leaves he may have walked around the market ten or fifteen times (and always, as it were, on his toes). If the market is outdoors, he is always on the lookout for selling dealers who have just pulled in in their vans and are unloading their stock. He will often head straight for a truck or van that is being emptied and buy a piece before it even hits the dewy morning air. If you want to compete with him, you will have to use his methods.

Flea and antiques markets are a fascinating part of the lifeblood of many dealers in country antiques, but there the sellers usually make no guarantees about the authenticity of what they are selling. You can get some fantastic bargains, but you can also get badly burned. Caveat emptor.

OTHER SOURCES

Tag sales, garage sales, and the like can also be sources of antiques, but rarely. Tag sales are usually carefully orchestrated to force you to dig through piles of junk elbow-to-elbow with people who are looking for a used toaster or an authentic Currier and Ives printed in 1952.

Garage sales can be better, even exceptional in the case of someone who is moving and selling part or all of an antiques collection. But here you may encounter another problem. The family does not want to move Great-uncle Herbert's sea chest that has been refinished to glisten like an ice cube. But, after all, it did belong to Great-uncle Herbert and has been passed down through umpty-ump generations. Just think of all the sentimental value it has. Just think, too, of how guilty the family is about selling it. So do not be surprised if

Great-uncle Herbert's chest and other pieces like it are priced far, far above their market value.

Finally, do not rule out newspaper classified advertisements as a source of antiques. Some ads may be dead ends, some may lead you to dealers, but others may end in a pot of gold. One ad I answered led me to an astounding private collection of country furniture owned by a woman who had just moved to a small house in Pennsylvania from a large house in Indiana. Among the pieces for sale were an eighteenth-century trestle table, a paneled seventeenth-century chest, and an Amish water bench—and those were just the items that she was storing in her basement!

ANTIQUE OR FAKE?—
WHAT TO LOOK FOR
3

In the antiques field, there are eight categories of objects you may hear collectors and dealers discussing: all-original pieces, pieces in the rough, restored pieces, monkeys, married pieces, reproductions, fakes, and imports. Any piece you see will fall into one or more of these categories. As you may have guessed, generally only the first three are desirable to a collector. You can determine what category a piece falls into through various general signs of age and authenticity. (There are also specific signs of age and authenticity that apply to the individual forms of furniture— chairs, tables, cupboards, etc. These are noted at the beginning of each chapter covering the particular form.)

An all-original piece is one whose component parts have never been changed in any way, except for normal wear and perhaps for minor recent or early repairs. Most collectors rightly insist that paint is a component part of any piece that was originally painted and that a paint-stripped piece is not all-original even if the rest of its parts are intact. Some also hope that the rush or splint seats of chairs will be original, but that is often wishful thinking. All-original condition is the most rarely found, most desirable, and, of course, the most expensive.

Restored pieces are common. In fact, it is unusual to find a piece of country furniture that has not been restored to its original (one hopes) appearance in some way. In this category, one or more parts have not simply been repaired but have been replaced where they have irreparably broken or have disappeared. The older the piece, the greater the likelihood that it has been restored in some way, and it is up to you to determine not only if a piece has been restored properly—if the restorations are right for the age and style of the piece—but also if the quality of workmanship is good. As for the quantity of restoration that should be tolerated, that will usually depend on a piece's age or rarity. There is little justification in buying an arrow-back rocking chair from the 1820s that has any restoration (although some repairs might be acceptable), but a banister-back chair from the 1720s could be only 80 percent original and still be relatively desirable. Paint is considered a part of a piece that can be restored and should be taken into account along with the wooden parts and the hardware.

A piece that is in the rough is one that is still in need of repair or restoration. Some dealers who are also restorers like buying pieces that are in the rough because they are cheaper than all-original and restored pieces. If you are good with wood or know someone who is, you might consider buying them, too, but remember to draw the line somewhere. A slat-back chair that has had rockers added to it that must be removed and that needs four new feet, one new slat, and a new rush seat is relatively easy and inexpensive to restore and might be worth it; a Windsor chair with a cracked bow, four broken spindles, cut-down legs, and a cracked seat might bankrupt you to restore (and would the final product be a restored antique or just a reconstruction with a few old parts?). On the other hand, many collectors buy pieces in the rough not to restore them but for their component parts. Some parts of early furniture, they feel, are so beautiful in themselves that they can be displayed like sculpture apart from the piece to which they were originally attached. And some collectors simply like to keep old furniture in "as found" condition, complete with broken parts and early repairs. You pay your money and take your choice.

A monkey, quite simply, is a piece that has been "monkeyed" with. Monkeying usually consists of adding parts to a piece to increase its market value, but monkeying can also mean subtracting parts. An example of monkeying by adding parts would be transforming a splay-leg tavern table into a butterfly table by adding a new oval top with drop leaves and adding the wing-shaped leaf brackets that give the butterfly table its name. On the other hand, if a monkeyer removed the two top doors from a four-door closed cupboard and then tried to make it appear as though it had always been an open, doorless cupboard, he would be monkeying by subtracting parts. Yet a buyer who was fooled by such monkey business would expect to pay more for this "second-generation" open cupboard than he would for the closed cupboard, because original open cupboards are rarer and usually earlier than cupboards with doors on top.

A married piece is a monkey on a giant scale. In this category are pieces of furniture that are made up of parts from two or more other pieces. A simple example of a marriage would be placing a hanging wall cupboard on a table and selling this new conglomeration as a secretary. Here is one case where a divorce could only be applauded.

A reproduction is, of course, a piece that is relatively new but has been constructed to look like an old form of furniture. Perhaps it has even been made from old wood. There is never any doubt that a reproduction is not an antique: the seller or maker will tell you, or there may be a label or brand on the piece attesting to its youth. "Repros" are not made to fool anyone. They exist so that people can purchase furniture that suits their home decor without paying the price of a genuine antique, although, ironically, some repros cost more than the real thing.

A fake can be a repro that is misrepresented as an antique. It can also be a piece that has been built from the ground up for the specific purpose of being sold as an antique. Actually, well-faked antiques, like good counterfeit money, are rare—the time, expense, and expertise that go into making them often do not justify the profit that can be made in selling them. Heavily restored pieces, monkeys, and married pieces are really no better than fakes.

Imported furniture is another problem for

the collector, but not a new one. In his *Furniture Treasury*, Wallace Nutting reported being cheated out of a considerable amount of money in the 1920s when he bought a Carver-style settee that turned out to have been made in Sweden. Today the problem is compounded by the fact that not only are "important" pieces of furniture being imported but so are pieces that resemble simple country furniture, especially from Spain. Canadian country furniture can also resemble American country furniture, although technically, I suppose, it is American. Since early American designs are based, in part, on foreign designs, it is sometimes difficult to distinguish an import from an American piece. Apart from a close examination of the woods used in construction to determine if they are consistent with those used in America, your only defense is a solid knowledge of how American pieces should and do look. If you have any doubts, don't write out a check.

FURNITURE WOODS

Antique country furniture was made in a wide variety of native woods and, on rare occasions, of an imported wood such as mahogany. It may come as a revelation to you that, more often than not, furniture was made of a combination of different woods rather than from a single wood.

For example, in case pieces of furniture—pieces such as chests of drawers that have a boxlike structure—the distinction is made between the primary and secondary woods from which they are constructed. The primary wood is what the outer, visible surfaces—such as the top, sides, feet, and drawer fronts of the piece—are largely made of; the secondary wood is what the insides—such as drawer sides, backs, and bottoms—are made of. While the secondary wood in a chest of drawers might be a commonly available, easily worked soft wood such as white pine or poplar, the primary wood might be a hard wood such as cherry, walnut, or maple. Those hard woods would virtually never be used as secondary woods; on the other hand, white pine might be used as both the primary and secondary woods on a given piece.

In case pieces, a combination of woods was used primarily for the sake of beauty and economy. But on some forms of furniture different woods were used because of their special structural characteristics. Windsor chairs are perhaps the premier example of this practice. Maple is one of the best woods to use for turning, since it is close grained and strong, allowing it to be turned with sharp edges and dramatic thicks and thins without breaking in normal use. Therefore, it was often used for the legs and arm supports of Windsor chairs. Pine does not turn very well, but since it is light and easy to shape by carving, it was often used for Windsor chair seats, which are usually scooped out to conform to the body. Hickory can be turned fairly well and also has elastic qualities that make it ideal for the thin, springy spindles in the backs of Windsors. Since oak can be steamed, bent to a rounded shape, and then clamped to hold that shape when it dries, it was often used for the bent bows and comb pieces of Windsors. (A Windsor chair so constructed would then have been painted to disguise the various woods and to meld them into an eye-pleasing unified design.)

Probably the most commonly found woods in country furniture are maple, walnut, cherry, birch, poplar, and white, or pumpkin, pine. Many others are found, too, including apple, ash, basswood, beech, butternut, cedar, chestnut, elm, gum, hickory, locust, oak, pear, northern yellow and southern hard pine, spruce, and sycamore. When maple (and, less frequently, cherry, walnut, or birch) logs are sawed into boards, they are sometimes discovered to have an attractive striped pattern, or figure, that runs across the normal wood grain. This is called tiger or curly maple, and it is highly prized. Maple is also found with a figure of dots across its surface; this is called bird's-eye maple.

An ability to recognize these woods can help you determine whether or not a piece is of American origin and if it has been properly restored. Maple, for example, is a distinctly American wood not found in early European furniture; hickory is also thought to be American; and while oak was used as a secondary wood on English furniture, it was probably never used that way in America. Although it has been tried by others, I do not feel that there is a meaningful way to describe in words how to distinguish one wood from another. White pine is relatively easy to identify since it is wide grained and soft, readily taking a fingernail impression. But even the experts are sometimes stumped by other woods and must resort to microanalysis of the cellular structure to distinguish, for example, walnut from cherry. The best way to acquire this important knowledge of woods is from experience with their appearance and textures. There are several books that contain color pictures of various woods; one of the less expen-

sive of these is published by the Forest Service
of the United States Department of Agriculture and is listed in the Further Reading section of this book.

DRESSED AND FINISHED WOOD

One of the first things you will notice about
the boards in many pieces of antique furniture
is that they are wide and thick. I own a Pennsylvania Windsor chair, circa 1760, whose poplar seat is 2 inches thick and 17 inches wide. A
tall New Jersey chest over drawers of mine,
circa 1820, has two backboards, one of which
is 22 inches wide; the boards on its sides are
1¼ inches thick.

Years ago trees were greater in diameter, so
many of the boards cut from them were, too.
Furthermore, lumber was not milled into
boards of uniform widths but was cut down as
needed by the furniture maker himself. Since
the backboards of a case piece might face the
wall, out of sight, the furniture maker did not
care about their uniformity and used them in
random widths.

A board that is an inch or more thick is almost certainly old, though if a board is less
than an inch thick it does not necessarily mean

that it is modern. However, today's lumber is milled to less than an inch, and a board that is really thin—say, a quarter of an inch or less—and has no obvious rough spots is surely machine dressed.

If you were to run your fingers over the underside of the Windsor chair seat or across the boards of the chest over drawers—against the grain—you would feel ripples. In the proper oblique light you could see these ripples. Another method of detecting them is to lay a straight edge across the grain of an old board and place a light behind it; the light will shine under the straight edge where there are shallow valleys in the board's surface. These ripples tell you that a board was hand smoothed along its grain with a jack plane, which has a blade with a curved nose. You will find them on genuine antiques, sometimes so pronounced that they could be called gouges, in such places as drawer bottoms, door panels, tabletops, plank seats, and chest boards. They will usually be more obvious on soft woods such as pine or poplar than on hard woods such as walnut or maple.

A pine Dutch cupboard of mine, circa 1800, has backboards that are rough to the touch, with parallel lines about an eighth of an inch apart running across the grain of the boards more or less perpendicular to their edges. The roughness of the boards and the parallel lines indicate that the boards were cut from the log with a pit or gang saw rather than with a circular saw. A pit saw has a long, straight blade that the sawyers moved up and down to cut the boards, one of them standing in a pit while the other stood atop the log. The water-powered gang saw is simply a multibladed variation of the pit saw that makes more than one cut with each pass of the blades. These saws left straight, parallel kerf, or teeth, marks on boards because they reciprocated up and down in a straight line. Straight kerf marks are often found on the backboards of pieces of furniture because those boards face the wall and further smoothing of them with a jack plane was considered unnecessary.

Circular saws, on the other hand, leave arched kerf marks across the surface of a board. The circular saw was first used in America about 1820 and almost exclusively after 1850. Thus a board with arched circular-saw marks must have been milled after 1820, while a board with straight pit- or gang-saw marks probably dates from before 1850.

Generally speaking, a piece constructed of boards with circular-saw marks should be looked on with suspicion since they indicate that a piece is late and was made by machinery. However, some desirable late pieces with circular-saw marks show other clear indications of hand manufacture.

WOOD COLOR

On the chest over drawers and the Dutch cupboard, all the boards in a given position are the same color; that is, all the backboards on the Dutch cupboard have the same dark gray tone; the insides of the chest's drawers are the same light hue. What does this mean?

Exposure to light, air, and dust changes the color of wood over the years, as does continual waxing or cleaning. Thus old wood does not look like new wood. It takes on a thin surface patina, characteristic of the particular wood, that is nearly impossible to fake and that is highly prized by collectors. Pine may turn brown if it has been waxed for many years, grayish-white if it has been scrubbed with soap and water, or almost black with age. Over time, maple will turn to honey yellow. Of course, the degree of color change depends on how much exposure the wood has had and for how long. While the exposed backboards of a case piece may be very dark, the enclosed drawers of the same piece may seem almost new. But whatever color the wood has become, one thing is certain: all wood of the same type that is located in the same position on a piece should show the same degree of color change. If the colors don't match, something has been replaced. The piece is not all original and should not be sold as such.

But why, you might ask, couldn't a restorer or faker fool you simply by using old wood, even though it is not original to the piece? First, because a faker would have to make sure that all the boards he was adding were exactly the same color, and those boards would be difficult to find. And second, because the boards would probably have to be cut down in some way to fit the piece, and the places where the saw was used—on the ends and edges of the boards, for example—would not be the same color as the rest of the board.

SIGNS OF HAND TURNING

Early lathes did not rotate very fast, and consequently it is not unusual—in fact, it is desirable—to find the marks of the turner's chisel on chair and table legs, bedposts, and other turned parts of antique country furniture. These marks are analogous to those left by the jack plane and appear as narrow gouges that spiral completely around the turning.

They are often more obvious in the narrow parts of turnings since a chisel with a thinner blade was used there, and, furthermore, it was more difficult to smooth out those parts. Also, because country furniture was often turned by eye, parts such as chair finials may differ considerably in thickness and height—another good indication of age.

Modern lathes leave marks at one end of a turning that look like a broken X. Such marks would, of course, be a clear indication of a fake or a replaced part.

SIGNS OF HAND MOLDING

Early molding was cut by hand with special molding planes. There are two types of molding: run-in and applied.

Run-in molding is cut directly on the edge of a board, such as around the edge of the top of a chest, and so it cannot project beyond or above the board on which it is cut. Applied molding is attached in separate strips, usually with brads or hardwood pins (for more on brads and pins, see the section below on Furniture Construction). Thus applied molding must project beyond the edge or surface of the board to which it is attached. It can even be attached in several layers of separate strips to build up a molding design that would have been very difficult to cut in one piece. Multiple layers of applied molding are often found in the cornices of such case pieces as cupboards and chests of drawers.

Although the molding cuts may appear to be straight when looked at from head on, hand-cut molding exhibits many irregularities. Its unevenness can be easily detected by placing your eye near one end of the molding and sighting along it. Machine-made molding will, of course, show no such unevenness.

This sighting test can also be used for hand-carved fluting, reeding, and chamfering.

SHRINKAGE

Wood shrinks across the grain as it loses moisture, and this unavoidable shrinkage can be an excellent indication of age. Shrinkage will cause age cracks to appear in boards. These occur first at the ends, which are sometimes severely split. Shrinkage will cause boards that originally butted against each other—in tabletops or on the back of a case piece, for example—to separate, leaving gaps between them. Even single-board tabletops that were once round will become elliptical, with a shorter diameter across the grain of the board than along the grain. Tabletops and leaves will warp from shrinkage; but when they have breadboard ends, something else may happen. As can be seen clearly in fig. 75, the breadboard ends on the leaf now project beyond the edge of the leaf, although they were flush with the leaf's edge when the table was made. This has happened because the leaf has shrunk across its grain, that is, across its width. However, since the grain of the breadboard ends is perpendicular to that of the leaf, they have shrunk in the opposite direction while retaining their original length. The same principle applies to desk lids that have breadboard ends.

Also, because of shrinkage, applied moldings that were once tacked flush with the edge of a board will tend to separate from it. And turnings that were once round will today be distinctly elliptical; this can be measured with calipers or sometimes felt with the fingers or detected by eye.

WEAR

Signs of wear will appear on country furniture on any parts that were subject to contact with other objects, such as walls, dustcloths, floors, parts of the human body, and moving parts of the same piece of furniture. Although evidence of wear does not necessarily indicate great age, you should always look for it. When you find it, ask yourself why it is there and if it appears in a logical place. If wear appears in an illogical place, you may be looking at a monkey, a marriage, or a fake. The same principle applies to *not* finding wear in a place where you would expect to find it.

Let's take a slat-back chair as a typical example of where you might look for wear. The front rung or rungs may be worn from continual contact with feet, more deeply toward the outside surfaces than at the center. If the chair has arms, they may be worn from the hands and arms of the people who used them. The insides of the back posts may show wear at the points where the shoulders rubbed against them (which would affect the depth of the scribe marks, as discussed below under Scribe Marks). The backs of the finials, especially on side chairs, may show wear from rubbing against a wall. The front and back edges of the front and rear feet, respectively, may be worn from having been dragged across the floor, and the bottoms of the feet will have dirt, cracks, and gouges in them (called dotage). Even the front edges of the tops of the front leg posts and finials or the entire length of the back posts may be worn if the chair was used as a kind of baby walker that was pushed across the floor by generations of toddlers. And if the chair has its original paint, that, too, will be worn away to the raw wood at any or all of the spots just discussed.

Wear may also be found in such places as the bottoms and sides of drawers, on the edges of cupboard doors that originally had no knobs and had to be opened with the finger-nails, on pine tabletops that were scrubbed daily for years with soap and water (scrub tops), on the stretchers of tables—even on the outside edges of a table leg where it may have been dusted for years (the inside edges may not be worn appreciably).

These signs of wear give country furniture much of its charm and value. Far from wishing to obliterate them by overzealous refinishing, or skinning, we should preserve them for the aura of authenticity they lend a piece of furniture. I do not wish to harp on this matter of refinishing, but I think the following quotes, taken from three books published twenty-six years apart, should drive the point home:

> "Once it was considered desirable to go to the bottom of all the old finish to make the piece 'look nice' . . . but the writer feels that a serious loss is thereby incurred. . . . Why does one wish to buy an old piece that looks

new?"—Wallace Nutting, *Furniture Treasury*, vol. 3 (1933)

"Excessive refinishing ruins more antiques than all other causes put together. . . . All the shellac in China will not restore the outer layer of wood, and nothing can repair the ravages of the rotary sander."—Moreton Marsh, *The Easy Expert in Collecting and Restoring American Antiques* (1959)

"An old surface is what makes an early piece different from a good copy. . . . We are so conditioned by colonial *kitsch* that it takes a leap of faith not unlike a conversion to see that a grungy, tattered, cracked and beat-up surface is marvelous. . . . To dislike it is the same as disliking the face of T. S. Eliot or Robert Frost in very old age."—John T. Kirk, *The Impecunious Collector's Guide to American Antiques* (1975)

PAINT

Much, if not most, early country furniture of all sorts was painted. This may come as a surprise to you if you have been brainwashed into thinking of the raw pine or maple look as somehow being the ultimate in "early Americana." The experienced collector knows better and, in fact, seeks out and is willing to pay more for pieces that carry their original painted surfaces—either on top or beneath later layers of paint that may be removed to reveal the original. Even if a piece has only traces of its original paint, it is worth more to a collector than one that has been totally stripped, for to him the old paint is as much a part of a piece's history, beauty, and charm as any other aspect of it—and sometimes more.

Country furniture—especially chairs, tables, beds, and those case pieces made of soft primary woods—was painted for a number of reasons: to beautify and protect it, to integrate the appearance of diverse woods into a unified design, to make one wood look like another (grain painting), and to use it as a vehicle for folk art. Red, black, and yellow were used from the seventeenth century onward. Slightly later almost any color you could think of was used, including green, black, brown, gray, and white. Blue is basically a nineteenth-century color, and the famous red, white, or gray milk paints were probably not used before the 1830s.

Differentiating old paint from new is not always easy, for there are professionals who are exceptionally skilled at restoring (or faking, if you will) the appearance of old paint. But as is the case with most good craftspeople today, they are few and far between. The irony in all this is that in the 1920s it was considered proper to strip off old paint, while today those stripped pieces are being repainted to please or fool collectors.

Here are a few guidelines to follow when examining paint. First, smell it! A piece that has been recently repainted often smells that way. New paint can sometimes be dented with the fingernail or other instrument; old paint usually cannot. When scraped with a metal blade, new paint is removed in ribbons while old paint may chip and sometimes disintegrate (unless it was applied like a stain in a very thin coat that has been absorbed by the wood). Old paint may become alligatored as the paint shrinks. Old paint is muted in color while new paint is relatively bright. Old paint will be worn away in places where a piece received the most use; new paint will not (assuming that the faker did not bother with details). Sometimes paint fakers do not work too carefully and allow their paint to drip; thus drip marks may indicate new work. Also, some fakers rub dirt or throw dust onto new paint to make it look old, but usually all they accomplish is to make the surface look dirty or gritty.

New paint can be used not only to fake the original surface appearance of a piece but also to disguise it. Paint can hide nails and screws and their holes that have been puttied over, repairs and replacements, and much more. I would never buy a piece that was covered by a heavy coat of late paint unless I was certain of its rightness or unless the dealer unconditionally guaranteed its authenticity. Many are the dealers and collectors I have known, including myself, who have been hoodwinked by new paint—usually only once.

Just because a piece has one or more layers of paint covering its original hue does not mean that you should immediately try to completely remove the top layers. Sometimes the effect of several layers of worn paint is very appealing, and sometimes it is simply impossible to remove the later layers in a way that will not smear the original paint. If you do decide to remove the later layers with a solvent or by light scraping, remember that red was often used as a *base* coat, so that the penultimate layer of paint may actually be the original top coat.

Paint over paint can also be advantageous. The various layers can tell you which parts of a piece have been replaced and which are original. If all the parts are original, when you carefully scrape away a small patch of paint each part should reveal the same layers of color in the same order, as though you had sliced through the piebald layers of an onion. If some of the parts do not have the same "paint history," or if they do not all end in the same base color, you may discover which parts are not contemporary with the others.

Even if a piece appears to have been stripped of its original paint, small traces of it may remain in such places as the grain of the wood, in turnings, in molding, in joints, and in places not normally visible such as the underside of a chair arm. If the parts all have traces of the same paint, they may all be original to the piece. Parts that do not have these paint traces may be replacements.

If the paint on a piece seems to be original, keep one other fact in mind: when the piece was first made, it probably had no obvious dents, cracks, or breaks in its wood and any applied molding was tacked flush to the surface behind it. If you find paint in cracks, areas where pieces of wood have separated from each other, or on parts where the paint should be worn away, such as chair rungs, it must have been applied *after* the defects or wear appeared and thus is not original.

Many collectors become euphoric over grain-decorated furniture. I do not mean poplar that has been stained to look like cherry but furniture with a trompe l'oeil paint grain. This was popular in the nineteenth century and was done in a number of ways—with the fingers, sponges, crumpled newspaper, combs, feathers, brushes, various solvents, even with candle smoke. Now viewed as a kind of folk art, grain-decorated pieces sometimes bring high prices. Whether you appreciate grain painting is a matter of your own taste, but do remember that softwood painted to resemble golden oak probably dates from the *late* nineteenth century, when that wood in its natural state became popular.

WORMHOLES

What we like to call wormholes in wood are actually made by insects, which seem to favor dining on walnut, chestnut, maple, oak, and fruitwoods but also attack pine and poplar. They appear as pinhead size dots on the surface of a board or turning. Below the surface, however, they do not follow a straight path but meander, much like ant holes. Wormholes are sometimes faked; to test their authenticity, experts may insert a thin wire into them, noting whether or not the wire bends (fake wormholes, of course, are straight).

Since their presence does not necessarily mean that a piece is old, in a sense it is irrelevant whether or not wormholes are real. More important is their overall appearance. Presumably, a furniture maker would virtually never use already wormy wood to construct a piece of furniture; therefore, the wormholes must be made *after* the piece is constructed. On the other hand, fakers and restorers sometimes do use old, already wormy wood. When they saw, plane, or turn this wood, their tools cut through the meandering worm tunnels and leave channels, as opposed to only small holes, on the surface. Thus worm channels are a cause for suspicion, since they often indicate that a part has been replaced or that an entire piece has been faked from old wood that was wormy *before* it was incorporated into a piece of furniture. However, it is possible that some original parts normally subject to wear, such as a chair stretcher or handhold, might become worn down to the worm channels.

Note, too, that wormholes can so seriously weaken a piece such as a chair that it becomes unusable.

FURNITURE CONSTRUCTION

If you wonder why so many pieces of early American furniture have survived in such good condition, consider this: some of the same construction methods have been found on Egyptian furniture dating from as early as 3000 B.C.—for example, mortise-and-tenon joints. These are tried and true methods in the extreme!

Joinery and cabinetmaking. In country furniture, the simplest, and in many ways the poorest, method of fastening two boards to each other is the butt joint (fig. A): the boards' ends are butted up against each other and then nailed together. This construction method is often found on six-board chests.

A. *Butt joint*

The disadvantages of the butt joint are many: the wood may shrink, thus opening the joint; the nails may back out of their holes in time; and since the boards are held rigidly, shrinkage can cause them to split seriously. Also, the joint is not "invisible" because the nails show on the surface unless their holes are puttied over and the piece is painted.

Rabbeting is a better method (fig. B). In the basic rabbet joint, an L-shaped cut is made along the edge of one board, which overlaps the end of the board to which it is joined. In constructing the sides of a drawer, this joint is stronger than the butt joint, and it can be

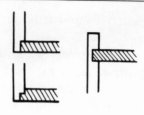

B. *Rabbet joints*

nailed from the side so that the nails are hidden when the drawer is closed. Seventeenth-century drawers were often made this way. Two other rabbet joints are shown in figure B.

Next, toward the end of the seventeenth century came dovetailing—triangular pieces cut at the end of one board that fit into triangular cutouts at the end of another board, like jigsaw puzzle parts. In the earliest drawers we find one or two wide, crude dovetails, sometimes with a nail hammered through them (fig. C). Some of these drawers may be rabbeted at the back but dovetailed at the front. When also dovetailed at the back, the dovetails

scribe mark

C. *Early eighteenth-century single dovetail*

sometimes project beyond the end of the drawer. By 1720 we find on drawers three or four narrower, but still quite wide, nonuniform dovetails that are more finely crafted than the earlier examples (fig. D). And later—1780 and beyond—many, but not all, drawer dovetails are very thin and fragile looking (fig. E).

Dovetailing may be found in many places on furniture—the sides of chests; the tops of chests of drawers; the ends of drawer blades, which separate the drawers from each other.

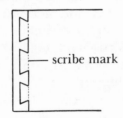

D. *Eighteenth-century dovetails*

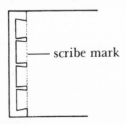

E. *Nineteenth-century dovetails*

Factory pieces may also have dovetailed drawers, but they are machine cut and easy to distinguish from the hand-cut variety. Machine-cut dovetails have no scribe marks along their edges (see the next section, Scribe Marks); also, they are all exactly the same size and are consequently regularly spaced, which is never the case with hand-cut dovetails.

Although you can date a handmade drawer with some certainty by the style of dovetailing used, dovetailing never replaced rabbeting and butt joining as a construction method in country furniture. Thus, just because a drawer is rabbeted together does not mean that it necessarily dates from the seventeenth century.

Joinery by mortise and tenon was used in all periods of American furniture construction and is extraordinarily durable (fig. F). In this joint, one or more tongue-shaped tenons are

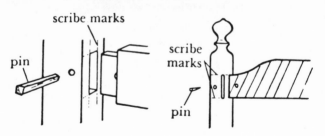

F. *Mortise-and-tenon joints*

cut at the end of a board, and they fit into corresponding holes, or mortises, in the other board. Sometimes the mortise hole is cut all the way through so that the end of the tenon is visible (open mortise), but more often the mortise is closed and the end of the tenon hidden. To secure a mortise-and-tenon joint, a hardwood pin is usually driven right through both pieces of wood in the joint. The pin may or may not project beyond the other side of the joint. In a joint with an open mortise, a wedge may be driven into the visible end of the tenon, thus spreading and holding it in place. Mortise-and-tenon joints are commonly found in the stretchers and legs of tables, on the skirts of tables and chests of drawers, on the slats and posts of slat-back chairs, and many other places.

Panel construction, made like a picture frame, is used to make such furniture parts as cupboard doors and the sides of some case pieces. Into a four-board frame is set a panel. The panel actually fits into narrow grooves that have been cut into the inside edges of the rails (the horizontal boards of the frame) and the stiles (the vertical boards), the edges of the panel having been beveled, or chamfered, so that they are thin enough to slide into the grooves. The stiles and rails are held together

G. *Chamfered drawer bottom rabbeted into drawer side*

with mortise-and-tenon joints. The advantages of panel construction are twofold: first, although the panel has been chamfered at the edges, it is thick in the middle and therefore strong; and second, since the panel only fits into the grooves in the rails and stiles but is not held totally immobile, it will not normally split from shrinkage. Although it is not called panel construction, the bottoms of drawers are usually chamfered and set into grooves in the sides and front of the drawer, just like a panel (fig. G). Panel construction was used on cupboard doors in all periods of furniture making. It was also used on the sides and fronts of seventeenth- and nineteenth-century case pieces, but hardly at all in the eighteenth century (which, by the way, is why many eighteenth-century case pieces with solid sides have badly split boards).

Butt, lap, tongue-and-groove, and spline joints were used to attach boards to each other edge-to-edge (fig. H). These joints are found in

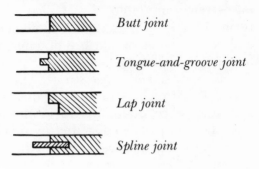

Butt joint

Tongue-and-groove joint

Lap joint

Spline joint

H

all periods on tabletops and backboards and in the nineteenth century on cupboard tops, drawer bottoms, and other places.

Country chairs usually have several parts that are socketed into other parts—for example, a chair rung socketed into a leg post—and the socket itself can tell you something about the age of the chair. Up through about 1840, socket holes were drilled with augers that had what is called a pod bit, which was not screwlike but straight with a rounded nose. Thus, if there were a way that you could see and feel inside the socket of a chair made before 1840—that is, if the rung could be pulled out of its socket—you would discover that the end of the socket was rounded. Around 1825, the screwlike auger with another, smaller start-

ing screw came into use. Called a gimlet-
pointed bit, it makes a socket whose end is flat
and at the center of which is another, smaller
hole made by the starting screw.

Pins, wedges, nails, and screws. The slats of
chairs, the stretchers of tables, paneled doors,
and other parts of country furniture are very
often held in place or together by small hardwood pins that are easy to see (fig. F). Although the lack of pins, especially in a paneled
door or a table, is not necessarily an indication
of inferior construction, it could be an indication of lateness (glue was not in general use
until about 1750 and was never used exclusively in the best furniture).

Why were pins used instead of nails? Because nails were expensive and pins worked
better in mortise-and-tenon joints.

Sometimes called trunnels (i.e., "treenails"),
these pins that may seem humble and un-
sophisticated are actually ingenious. Whether
they are tapered or not, pins are never round
in cross section but square or polygonal. They
were made this way so that their relatively
sharp edges would bite into the round holes
into which they were driven, helping to secure
them. Round pins that look like dowels are
thus an indication of a fake or a poor restoration. Although when a piece was first made the

pins were driven home flush with the wood surrounding them, as time passed the wood around them shrank and the pins tended to be squeezed out of their holes. On genuine antiques the old pins may project from the surface a sixteenth of an inch or more; pins that are flush with the surface are either new or indicate that the piece has been improperly refinished.

It is a fairly well-established fact that pins were often applied through mortise-and-tenon joints in what is called the draw-bore method. The hole in the mortise was drilled slightly farther out than the hole in the tenon, so that, when the tenon was socketed into the mortise, the holes through them did not quite line up. When the pin was hammered through the joint, it would draw the tenon into the mortise to make an exceedingly tight joint. This may explain why pins, when removed from a joint, are often found to have a slight kink in them.

Wedges are so effective in furniture construction that today you will find them in high-quality designer furniture. In antique country furniture perhaps their most notable use is in the spindles, arm supports, and legs of Windsor chairs. For example, a chisel cut is made in the top of a leg, and a wedge-shaped piece of hardwood is inserted partway into the cut (fig.

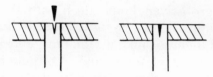

I. *Wedge joint*

I). The leg is then inserted into a hole drilled all the way through the chair seat and the wedge is hammered home. This expands the end of the leg, making a tight joint. If you look at the exposed end of any wedge joint from the top, you will notice that the wedge is always more or less at a right angle to the grain of the wood surrounding it (fig. J). The effect of this is to exert tremendous force on the wood around the wedged joint without splitting the wood along the grain. A wedge joint in which the wedge is not at right angles to the grain may indicate that the restoration has been made improperly or that the wedged part has been removed and replaced incorrectly.

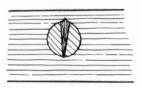

J. *Wedge joint from above*

Some pieces have wedges you cannot see—blind wedges. They are most often used where two pieces of hardwood are joined, for example, the legs and seat of an all-maple Windsor chair where the legs do not completely penetrate the seat. It works like this: a hole is bored partway through the seat; the wedge is inserted partway into the top of the leg; then the leg is hammered into the seat, thus driving home the wedge inside the hole.

Nails were used to hold many parts of country furniture in place, including tabletops, the sides and backboards of cupboards, and all the boards in six-board chests. From the seventeenth century probably through the early nineteenth century, nails were hand-forged from exceptionally pure iron, giving them certain distinctive qualities. They are very rust resistant; they bend relatively easily yet break infrequently; they are square in cross section and taper on all four sides to a sharp point; and they show the rough marks of the forger's hammer. Hand-forged nails range in size from tiny brads used for applying molding up to common nail length. They may have flat, bumpy "rose" heads, or square heads, or they may be headless. Since they were handmade, no two of them are alike.

Some experts say that any piece with its

original hand-forged nails can be dated before 1790, the approximate date when machine-made, cut nails were introduced. But I would give more leeway than this—say, 1820 to 1825—since the thrifty country furniture maker probably saved his expensive hand-forged nails for later use. Boxes of such nails in pristine condition still turn up and are usually immediately devoured by restorers. I myself own a country tripod stand, circa 1820, whose legs are attached to the standard with hand-forged rose-head nails.

Machine-cut nails somewhat resemble hand-forged nails, but even cursory inspection will reveal significant differences. Like hand-forged nails, cut nails are square in cross section but taper on only their two opposite sides to a blunt, squared-off point; they tend to rust; they never have rose heads; and nails of the same size all look more or less alike. If you examine a cut nail closely, you may see shallow, parallel ridges, or burrs, running perpendicular to its edges—marks left by the cutting machine. A piece constructed with cut nails is virtually always nineteenth century.

Both hand-forged and cut nails are made as reproductions and are sometimes used to give the appearance of old construction. In addition, authentic old cut nails may be used for fakery. But even after nails have been hammered into place, there are ways of detecting their age or authenticity. Unless they have been really individually hand forged—which is very unlikely—the bumps in the heads of repro rose-head nails will all be identical. Also, a repro rose-head nail has a squared-off end like a cut nail, whereas the real thing tapers to a point. Thus, if they are at all exposed, examining the ends of repro rose-head nails should be another method of detecting fakery. In the case of cut nails, their exposed square heads are often found in furniture—especially in the backboards of case pieces—in rusted condition. Presumably, however, the nails were clean before they were hammered in, and the heads rusted in place. On the other hand, authentic old cut nails used for fakery are often found completely rusted, and the faker simply hammers them in. But he usually neglects the fact that when nails rust in place, the wood around the heads also becomes rust stained. If the nailheads are rusted but the wood around them is clean, your suspicions should be aroused. Finally, nails that have been in place for a long time take on a distinctive appearance that is fairly easy to recognize. The exposed wood that was splintered away when the nails were hammered in tends to darken, and the wood shrinks around—and sometimes slightly over—the heads, leaving no gaps. Thus new, raw wood or gaps around nailheads mean recently applied nails.

About 1870, modern, roundheaded, steel-wire nails were introduced. Needless to say, a piece constructed entirely with them is of doubtful value as an antique.

Screws, like nails, have been around for a long time—since perhaps as early as 1700. Like nails, they will tell you something about the age of a piece only if they are original to it. Handmade screws were doubtlessly more expensive and in shorter supply than nails, and so they are not often found on country furniture. The earliest screws are half an inch long or less; their threads are uneven, widely spaced, and rounded on the edges; their heads are always flat and not quite round, with a screwdriver slot that is narrow, shallow, and off center; and their tips are flat.

There is some controversy about when the first machine-cut screws were introduced. The consensus is about 1815, although some experts date them as early as 1785. In appearance they are somewhat like handmade, flat-tipped screws, but they are longer, their threads are more regular and sharp, and their heads are more nearly round. About 1850, the sharp-pointed, gimlet-end screws similar to the ones used today were introduced.

SCRIBE MARKS

Early furniture makers did not use pencils to mark off their work but instead used various tools with sharp points to actually inscribe thin, shallow grooves in the wood. These scribe marks may thus be an indication of early hand manufacture.

Among other things, scribe marks were used to mark the points of attachment of round furniture parts into sockets, the size and location of mortise holes, and the depth of dovetail cuts (figs. C, D, E, and F). Therefore, you should expect to find them in such places as the points where chair rungs are socketed into the legs (single scribe marks running around the legs), the points where chair slats fit into the back posts (usually two marks for each slat running around the posts), table legs where a stretcher and/or skirt is attached (usually rectangular marks delimiting the exact size of the mortise), and the edges of drawers along the dovetails (single marks).

Some scribe marks are also ornamental and so are deeper and wider than the usual marks. These are most often found in the center of the side stretchers of Windsor chairs where the medial stretcher is socketed. On Windsors with bamboo-turned legs, the bamboo ringing itself serves as scribe marks for the attachment of the stretchers.

The lack of scribe marks where you would expect to find them may indicate late or factory manufacture or replaced parts, the latter especially if some parts have scribe marks and others do not.

HARDWARE

Hardware is a term that can apply to wooden knobs found on country furniture as well as metal hinges and drawer pulls. Since hardware is easily removed and replaced, it will not tell you anything about the age or authenticity of a piece unless it is original to it. Keep in mind, too, that a complete set of eight Chippendale brasses may be worth more than the piece to which they are attached. Thus the temptation to remove and resell them separately, like cutting up a diamond into smaller stones, is sometimes overwhelming.

Hinges. Like nails and screws, early hinges were hand-forged. Hinges are often conveniently divided into the following categories: cotter-pin, butterfly, strap, ornamental, forged butt, and cast butt.

K. *Cotter-pin hinge*

The hand-forged iron cotter-pin hinge (also called a staple, clinch, or snipe hinge) is the simplest and perhaps the earliest (fig. K). Cotter-pin hinges are made from two iron rods about ⅙ to ⅛ inch thick. The ends of the rods are pounded to sharp points, then each is bent into a hairpin shape and linked together. The two parts of the hinge were inserted into holes in furniture parts. The protruding sharp ends were then spread apart and pounded back, or clinched, into the wood around them. These hinges were not very durable and often broke in use, so that frequently the only remaining evidence of them are the single holes their ends passed through and the two smaller holes and V-shaped marks where they were clinched. Cotter-pin hinges were used on chest lids, cupboard doors, and table leaves from about 1700 to about 1760, but they have been found on the lids of chests that date from as late as about 1820.

The hand-forged iron butterfly hinge, also used from about 1700 to 1760, takes its name from its resemblance when open to the out-

L. *Butterfly hinge*

spread wings of a butterfly (fig. L). Hand-forg-
ing causes butterfly hinges to be thicker in the
center than at the edges. And because each
half of the hinge has actually been folded and
hammered around the pin on which it pivots,
a separation often occurs with age along the
seam at the edges of the hinge. Butterfly
hinges were attached to the undersides of
table leaves and to the outsides of cupboard
doors with hand-forged screws or with
washers and rosehead nails, which were sometimes clinched back through the wood.

The hand-forged iron strap hinge, used
from about 1720 through perhaps 1840, is
made like a butterfly hinge and looks like one
or two tapering straps that usually end in an
arrow, circle, fleur-de-lis, or other shape (fig.
M). Commonly found on chest lids, they were

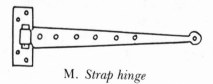

M. *Strap hinge*

usually attached with screws or with large, round-topped rivets to both the inside and outside of furniture, but not on table leaves.

Ornamental, or decorative, hand-forged iron hinges comprise the H, HL, and rattail varieties, terms nicely descriptive of their appearance (fig. N). In use from about 1700 through the early nineteenth century, they were attached with nails, screws, or both to the outside of cupboard doors. Like the strap hinge, they may be topped off with various shapes. A feature of the rattail hinge is that the socket (gudgeon) on the part attached to the cupboard door simply slides over the pin (pintle) on the part attached to the door frame, enabling the door to be easily lifted off the cupboard. H, HL, and LL hinges were made in brass as well as iron, but the brass varieties are rarely found on country furniture.

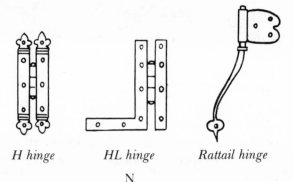

| *H hinge* | *HL hinge* | *Rattail hinge* |

N

Because they were tightly attached and because over the years wax and dirt builds up around them, butterfly, strap, and ornamental hinges tend to leave an outline of their shapes on the wood where they were attached. Thus even if a piece's hinges have been removed and replaced, you can often tell what they originally looked like.

Hand-forged iron butt hinges, squared off at the ends, were used from the early eighteenth century through about 1820, mainly on drop-leaf tables (fig. O). Cast-iron butt hinges appeared about 1815 and were used on tables and on the inside of cupboard doors, although

O. *Butt hinge*

some country craftsmen had the amusing habit of attaching them to the outside of the doors following the practice with the earlier ornamental hinges. Butt hinges are almost always set into shallow mortises in wood, and so if they have been removed, some evidence of these mortises will remain, either the mortises themselves or oblong wooden plugs filling the mortises.

Although the hinges just discussed are the most commonly found types, there are definitely others. I own a drop-leaf table that has hand-forged iron hinges whose ends are three-sided. Card tables may have special brass hinges attached to the ends rather than the undersides of their leaves. And some pieces even have leather hinges.

Knobs and brasses. Wooden knobs are found on country furniture from the earliest times to the latest. In fact, you are more likely to find a wooden knob of one style or another than any other kind of opening device. The earliest knobs are hardwood and date from the seventeenth century through about 1730. Longer than they are wide and ranging in length from 1 inch to 1¾ inches, they were attached in several different ways: they may simply have been driven into a hole of smaller diameter than their shanks; they may be held by a wooden peg through a hole in their shanks; or they may be nailed in place from the inside. Later wooden knobs are wider than they are long and so are called mushroom knobs. They may be attached in the old ways, or screws may have been driven into them from the rear. Some hardwood knobs dating from about 1830 and later are attached from the rear with thick, threaded softwood screws.

Before the Revolution, all furniture brasses,

or mounts, were probably imported from England. The earliest of these, the teardrop pull, is found on some country pieces (fig. P). Teardrop pulls are composed of a small, thin backing plate and a drop like a tiny door knocker.

P. *Teardrop pull*

The backing plate may have a pierced or tool-stamped (not engraved) geometric design. The drop itself is either flat or hollowed out in the back. The backing plate and drop are held in place by a single flat cotter pin that is usually clinched into the wood behind it. These mounts were not very durable and so only their telltale traces may remain: a single hole (that may have a later wooden plug in it) through which the cotter pin passed; the outline of the backing plate; and the two clinch holes on the inside of the pieces. If you find evidence that a piece once had teardrop pulls, or if it still has them, it can be safely dated from about 1670 to 1735.

Q. Cotter-pin bail handle

The popularity of teardrop pulls declined rapidly, and they were replaced (and overlapped in time) by cotter-pin bail handles—simply free-swinging handles held by two cotter pins that penetrate a thin, decorative backing plate (fig. Q). The ends of a bail handle are formed into little knobs, which keep them from slipping out of the cotter-pin eyelets, and the geometric designs are tool stamped. Cotter-pin bail handles were used from about 1700 to 1760.

The idea of using cotter pins to hold brasses was superseded about 1730, when hand-filed threaded bolts were introduced. The earliest bolted brasses are called bat's wing mounts (fig. R). Used from about 1730 to 1750, the

R. Bat's wing mount

bulbous bolt heads are drilled all the way through so that the ends of the handles are visible. The rest of the bolt is actually square down to where the threads begin, and the nuts, made from pieces of scrap brass, are not quite round. The slightly later bat's wing mounts (sometimes called early willow mounts), used as late as about 1810, have bolt heads that are drilled only about three-quarters of the way through, the ends of the handles being hidden (fig. S). Willow mounts were used exclusively on Chippendale furniture from about 1755 to 1810 (fig. T). Another type of Chippendale brass does not have a single large backing plate but two small

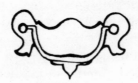

S. *Bat's wing, or early willow, mount*

T. *Willow mount*

round or oval "rosettes" behind each bolt head (fig. U).

If there are geometric designs on any of the brasses mentioned thus far, they will be tool stamped. Furthermore, all these brasses will have rough sand-casting marks on their back sides and will show the marks of the finishing file on their front sides, especially on the edges.

After about 1790, brasses were no longer cast but were stamped out of one piece of sheet brass, any ornamentation on them being in relief. The Hepplewhite types, used from about 1790 to 1830, are oval (fig. V). From about 1800 to 1830, large, round, hollow brass

U. *Rosette mount*

V. *Oval mount*

knobs sometimes called rosette knobs were used on both Hepplewhite and Sheraton pieces (fig. W). These knobs have their bolts permanently soldered in place. Oblong and polygonal brasses were used on Sheraton pieces from about 1810 to 1840, as were brasses shaped like lion's heads with ring pulls.

W. *Rosette knob*

Other late knobs and handles were made from all sorts of materials—glass, ceramic, brass, wood, steel, copper alloy—in a wide variety of shapes and sizes.

Here are a few more things to keep in mind about brasses. First, they are always meant to be highly polished, but perhaps what John T. Kirk calls "colonial *kitsch*" has led many people to think that old brasses should be left tarnished, as so many cheap reproductions are made. That, to me, is tantamount to purposely making stale bread. Second, when polished, early brasses are quite light in color. After about 1755, brasses were made with a higher copper content, which made them darker and more reddish. Third, like hinges, brasses tend to leave their outline on the front of a piece because wax and dirt accumulate around them over the years. This buildup is very evident around almost any brass that has been in place for a long time; and if the brass is removed, not only will its outline remain on the wood but the wood that was behind the brass will be lighter in color than the surrounding wood (and, of course, unmarked). Fourth, dating a piece from its original brasses can be productive, but because brasses could be stockpiled by a furniture maker, a piece might easily have brasses from a period earlier than its construction. Conversely, when a new shape of brass became popular, it may have been used on a style of furniture that is earlier than the brasses themselves. For example, it is not unusual to find oval Hepplewhite brasses on Chippendale-style country furniture. (More on periods and styles of furniture in the next chapter.) And finally, the decorative brasses that surround keyholes, called escutcheons, made in the same shapes as their companion handles, were not subject to the constant tugging that the handles were. Thus many pieces have replaced or missing handles but their original escutcheons. Obviously, then, the age of the escutcheons should be used in dating the piece.

By the way, one test for real, though not necessarily old, brass is that it is not magnetic.

PERIODS
AND STYLES OF
AMERICAN FURNITURE
4

Suppose someone placed before you a photograph of an automobile made in the 1920s and a photograph of one made last year, and he then asked you which car was made earlier. You would have no trouble telling him. Certain design features of the earlier auto—such as its boxiness, clamshell fenders, running boards, skinny tires, and enormous headlights—would immediately spark your recognition of it. If you really knew your stuff, you could arrange in chronological order a whole series of photographs of cars from different years because you would know when each style was popular.

Well, as you may have already guessed, it's the same with furniture. Styles came and styles went. When a style came, a furniture period began; when it went, the period ended (and another began). And if you knew when a certain style was popular, you could date a piece of furniture made in that style with some accuracy.

Continuing the car analogy, authentic Model T Fords were made during the Model T period (1908–27). If you bought a good copy of a Model T made in 1970, it would undoubtedly be in the Model T *style,* but it would not be authentic because it would not have been made in the Model T *period.* Similarly, you could buy a Queen Anne-style chair at a department store tomorrow, but it would not be a real Queen Anne chair because, as they say in the antiques world, it would not be "of the period," and its style would be pretty meaningless as far as dating it was concerned.

In other words, the beginning and ending dates of American furniture periods are derived from the time spans when certain styles were popular in America. But a furniture style is not the same as a furniture period.

Here are the names and approximate dates of the furniture periods most often used when country furniture is discussed. (If you hear or read about one not listed here, please look it up in the Glossary of this book.) You will notice that the dates of the periods overlap each other because styles did not go out of fashion overnight. Also, the styles of some forms of furniture—notably chairs, and to a lesser extent other forms—tended to remain popular longer in the country than in the more fashion-conscious urban areas. Hence, country furniture periods lasted longer than high-style, urban furniture periods with the same names. The later ending dates for country furniture periods are given in parentheses:

Early seventeenth century:	*1640–80*
Late seventeenth century:	*1670–1710*
William and Mary:	*1690–1735 (1800)*
Queen Anne:	*1730–60 (1810)*
Chippendale:	*1755–95 (1820)*
Hepplewhite:	*1790–1815 (1840)*
Sheraton:	*1800–1840 and later*

Next, here are a few of the distinctive design features of each furniture period. In case you did not know it, the Chippendale, Hepplewhite, and Sheraton periods are named after those three English furniture designers, whose ideas were reinterpreted and usually simplified in America. Some of the stylistic features that follow may be found on many of the pieces in this book, and figure numbers of representative examples are given in parentheses. The Style Index of this book will provide you with more examples. If some of the terms used are unfamiliar to you, please look them up in the Glossary.

Seventeenth century: General massiveness of proportions; stile feet (fig. 88); panel construction (fig. 88); decoration by applied ornament (fig. 94) or shallow carving (fig. 88); oak used as the primary wood in case pieces.

William and Mary period: Lighter, more vertical proportions; Spanish feet (fig. 12) and ball feet (fig. 96); block turnings (fig. 139) and bold turnings with dramatic thicks and thins (fig. 97); heavy applied molding (fig. 97); decoration on some case pieces by thick veneer and on some chairs with deep, pierced carving; walnut, maple, and birch the primary woods.

Queen Anne period: Still lighter and more vertical proportions; simple bracket feet (fig. 92) and cabriole legs with some variation of a pad foot (fig. 73); reverse curves in chair splats, crest rails, back posts, seats, and legs (the back of fig. 12); decoration by shell carving or a variation of it; lipped drawers; cherry, walnut, and maple the primary woods.

Chippendale period: Somewhat broader overall proportions than the Queen Anne style; more elaborately scrolled bracket feet (fig. 104) and heavier cabriole legs, sometimes with claw-and-ball feet; more squarish shapes, especially in the untapered, square legs of certain chairs and tables (figs. 17 and 74); chairs with pierced splats (fig. 16) and ladders (fig.

17); crest rails with ears (fig. 16); block or serpentine fronts on some case pieces; cock-beading on the case around flush drawers; mahogany, cherry, walnut, and maple the primary
woods.

Hepplewhite period: Thinner, somewhat boxy
proportions; neoclassical shapes, such as urns
(fig. 19); tapered square legs (fig. 65) that may
end in spade feet (fig. 106); French feet with
valanced skirts on case pieces (fig. 131); serpentine shapes on case pieces (fig. 113), tabletop edges (fig. 76), etc.; inlay; cock-beading
around the fronts of flush drawers; same
woods as the Chippendale period.

Sheraton period: Except in chairs, more
rounded, less boxy shapes; round, sometimes
tapering, legs with reeding, fluting, or lots of
rings and reels (fig. 66); tulip-shaped or but-
tonlike feet (fig. 66); same woods.

I sincerely hope that all this sounds relatively simple up to this point, because it is.
However, there are a few subtleties that are
important to understand.

First, styles do not work like bell curves,
climbing to an apex of design excellence and
then declining. Rather, they tend to come into
existence in their most fully developed form.
Subsequently, the trend over time is toward
lightness, thinness, simplification, and general

degradation until one style is superseded by another. Thus, for example, the thick ring turnings on the back posts of early eighteenth-century New England slat-back chairs (fig. 2) become progressively thinner (fig. 4) until they disappear completely in the nineteenth century (fig. 24); the dynamic baluster-and-ring turnings on the legs of mid-eighteenth-century Windsor chairs (fig. 30) become the far simpler bamboo turnings (fig. 31), which, in turn, become simply shallow, incised rings in the nineteenth century (fig. 37).

Second, styles of two or more different periods are often combined in country furniture, which is why it is a rule of thumb always to *date a piece by its latest stylistic feature.* Take, for example, figs. X and Y.

Fig. X somewhat resembles fig. 72: both have round tops and a fairly deep skirt (although fig. 72's skirt is scrolled), but the legs are obviously entirely different. The leg turnings on fig. X are more like those on figs. 87 and 116, which date from about 1820 to 1840 and are in the Sheraton style. Since the leg turnings are fig. X's latest stylistic feature, it must be dated accordingly.

Fig. Y resembles fig. 12, especially in its back, although the front stretcher is less boldly turned. But there is something odd about fig. Y, as though the maker had misunderstood

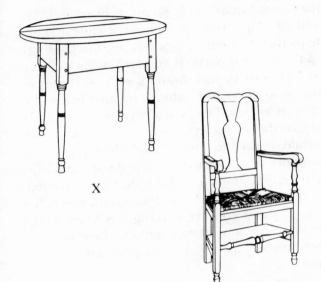

X

Y

the Queen Anne style or was trying to fit it
into a different standard of taste. Fig. Y's crest
rail does not have the graceful curves of fig.
12's crest rail; instead, there are two distinct
humps that run into notches on either side of
a perfectly flat center section—conceptually,
perhaps, not far removed from the crest rail
of fig. 40. The baluster shape of fig. Y's splat
appears to be moving downward, having
"slipped " about 3 inches, whereas the move-
ment of fig. 12's splat is upward. Fig. Y's feet

have that "tulip" look reminiscent of figs. 20 and 87. The arms are somewhat clumsy. Perhaps the most telling features are the turnings of the arm supports. If you look at such pieces as figs. 4 or 9, you should see the difference: on those chairs, the baluster turning below the arms is long and ends in a narrow ring directly above the front legs. Generally speaking, we would expect to find a similarly shaped arm support on a country Queen Anne armchair. On fig. Y, however, the baluster is stunted, and, more important, a superfluous, somewhat exaggerated concave turning has been added below it. When taken together, these features lead me to date fig. Y as early nineteenth century.

What about fig. 12 itself? It has a William and Mary-style base, which could easily be found on banister-back chairs like figs. 9 to 11, but its back is in the Queen Anne style. This chair not only combines styles from two different periods, as did figs. X and Y, but the periods are *contiguous.* That fact might lead you to the not unreasonable conclusion that fig. 12 exhibits a transition between the William and Mary and the Queen Anne periods— that the chair was made at a time when neither style was predominant but tastes were in the process of changing. And, indeed, some authorities have called pieces like fig. 12 "transitional." The implication of labeling fig. 12 transitional is that it could be dated quite early—say, at the very beginning of the Queen Anne period, possibly earlier. That, of course, might make fig. 12 expensive.

In fact, however, fig. 12 is almost certainly *not* transitional—very few, if any, country pieces are. What has probably happened in pieces such as fig. 12, as John T. Kirk has pointed out, is that the back of the chair has simply been updated to reflect the latest style trend, while the base has not. More evidence to support the "updated" rather than "transitional" idea is in the fact that many chairs have bases just like fig. 12 but backs like fig. 16—that is, William and Mary bases but Chippendale backs! Since the William and Mary period is not contiguous to the Chippendale period, there is no way that such a chair could be called transitional. The only other possibility is that the back has been updated.

Third, some distinctive forms of furniture actually developed during specific periods and did not even exist before them. Such a form is the chest on chest, as in fig. 103. This form was created during the Chippendale period—that is, there were no chests on chests before about 1755—and that fact is noted in the dates in parentheses for fig. 103, as it is for all other forms illustrated in Chapters 6 through 13.

Fourth, some forms of furniture, although they may have hints of other styles mixed in, were really made in only one style. Thus, for example, it would be redundant to say, "That is a William and Mary [-style] banister-back chair," since there is no other kind. On the other hand, banister-back chairs were such a popular form that they were made as late as about 1800. So, if the chair being discussed is one of the great early chairs actually made during the William and Mary period—1690–1735—rather than much later, you could say, "That is a period banister-back chair," and the point would be made.

Finally, many pieces simply cannot be categorized as to style. Slat-back chairs, made from about 1680 to 1840 and later, are a good example. We can often estimate when they were made—that is, during what period—and we might possibly say that a certain chair has certain stylistic elements from some period, but we would never state, for example, "That is a Queen Anne slat-back chair," since no such animal exists.

PRICES
5

The cost of country furniture varies widely from place to place, dealer to dealer, auction to auction. It depends not only on supply and demand but on many other factors as well. The following are some of the reasons that may cause antiques dealers to raise the price of a piece relative to other pieces of the same form and may cause collectors to pay more. You will have to decide for yourself, but I feel that the first twelve items are to one degree or another rational, the others less so:

1. Design interest (excellence, quaintness, etc.);
2. Surface interest, including paint;
3. Structural condition or "rightness";
4. Excellence of construction;
5. Rarity of form or design;
6. Uniqueness of design;
7. Age;
8. Primary wood used in construction, e.g., a piece in tiger maple as opposed to one in plain maple;

9. Regional interest (collectors often pay more for a piece made in the region where they live);

10. Usefulness, e.g., a hutch table with a widely overhanging top is more useful than one without it because you can sit closer to the table before banging your knees against the hutch;

11. Excellence of restoration;

12. Pieces in sets, e.g., a matching highboy and lowboy, a set of chairs;

13. The maker's brand, label, or initials on the piece;

14. The date of construction or of paint decoration on the piece;

15. The piece is being sold from a well-known collection or is known to have once been part of it;

16. Probable attribution of a piece to a certain maker even though no brand, label, or initials are present;

17. The piece has been "published" in an antiques book or periodical;

18. Historical associations, e.g., George Washington's Windsor chair;

19. Demand regardless of supply.

In spite of all this, I have tried to develop a very broad and flexible code for the prices you might expect to pay for certain pieces. This code, which appears at the end of the descriptive text for each form in Chapters 6 through 13, applies to the time of publication of this book. It is hoped that it will give you a good idea of the *relative* prices of the various pieces.

Here it is:

Code	From	To
V. inexp.	$1	$50
Inexp.	$50	$200
Mod. exp.	$200	$500
Exp.	$500	$1,000
V. exp.	over $1,000	

Chris Huntington, a well-known young New England antiques dealer, has said, "Out there somewhere is the finest of its kind at a bargain price," and I think he's right. If you will keep your eyes and ears open and be at the right place at the right time, and if you are, as John T. Kirk has put it, a "Sherlock Holmes of furniture," you should uncover a number of pieces in the inexpensive and moderately expensive categories.

So take heart, have fun—and make sure your bank book is balanced!

Part II

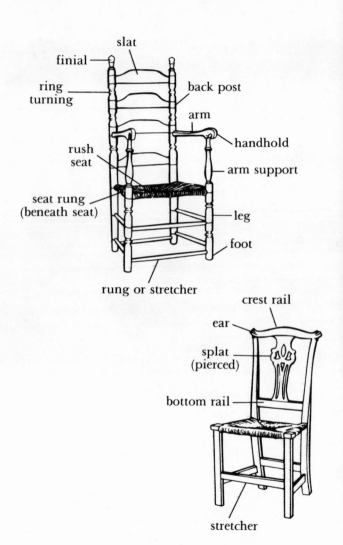

slat

finial

ring
turning

back post

arm

handhold

rush
seat

arm support

seat rung
(beneath seat)

leg

foot

rung or stretcher

crest rail

ear

splat
(pierced)

bottom rail

stretcher

CHAPS
6

CONSTRUCTION

Rush- or splint-seat chairs. These chairs have four seat rungs shaped like airplane wings in cross section, with the leading edge facing outward. The seat rungs are socketed either into all four leg posts, as in fig. 13, or into the back posts and into blocks that sit atop the front legs, as in fig. 12. The box framework formed by the seat rungs is wider in the front of the chair than in the back, and the seat is woven around it. The seat itself adds a great deal of structural strength to the chair.

In Carver chairs, the turned parts may be made with roughly shaped dowel ends whose sharp edges bite into the round sockets, holding them tightly. The rungs are often pinned and on some chairs completely penetrate the legs.

In slat-back chairs, the slats are mortised into the back posts, and one or more of the slats are almost always pinned. In late chairs square nails may be used instead of pins. Arms that roll over the front posts are usually pinned. Arms that are socketed into the front posts are often not pinned. The rungs are almost never pinned but may be held fast by blind wedges.

Banister-back, Queen Anne, Chippendale, and Hepplewhite chairs have mortised or socketed crest rails that are frequently pinned through the back posts. The vertical banisters or splats are mortised into the crest and bottom rails; banisters are not pinned, but splats often are. Spanish feet are sometimes made in two pieces that are glued together to form the carved outward scroll of the foot.

Slip-seat chairs. These Queen Anne, Chippendale, and Hepplewhite chairs are similar in construction to their rush-seat counterparts. In addition, they have removable upholstered or rush seats that rest on corner blocks. The seat rails are mortised and are usually pinned through the legs. The seat-rail mortise through the back legs may be open. The stretchers are mortised and are usually pinned to the legs; a setback, medial stretcher may be dovetailed into the side stretchers.

Plank-seat chairs. These nineteenth-century chairs have seats made of a single piece of wood. All parts are socketed or mortised together. Back and arm posts almost always penetrate the seat and are wedged, but the legs do not penetrate the seat. Arms that roll over the front posts are usually wedged. Crest rails are sometimes pinned from the back or wedged from the side; on late chairs, square nails may be used instead of pins.

Rocking chairs. Rockers on the earlier chairs are set into mortises in the legs, where they are pinned from the side. In late chairs square nails or screws may be used instead of pins. On the later chairs, the legs are socketed into the rockers, and they may be wedged.

EXAMINATION CHECKLIST

1. Has the chair lost some of its original height? The distance from the floor to the top of the seat on chairs with their full height is usually 17 or 18 inches.

2. Have the legs been pieced out? Examine the legs for any seams, color differences, and wood grain variations, especially near turnings or below the lowest stretcher. Look at the bottom of the feet for a dowel that goes through the new foot and anchors it into the leg above.

3. If the feet seem original, do they have the proper dotage?

4. If the chair has rockers, are they original to the chair or were they added at a later date?

The paint history of the rockers and the rest of the chair should jibe. Also, when chairs are cut down and rockers are then added, the rungs are almost always too close to the bottoms of the feet. The distance from the front rung to the bottom of the front leg on an original rocking chair is about 3½ inches, from the side rungs about 5 inches.

5. Are the front and back legs original? Do they jibe, respectively, in tool marks, age, wear, color, and paint history? Are they slightly out of round (a sign of age)? (Even square legs shrink across the grain.)

6. Especially on turned chairs, are there scribe marks where parts are mortised or socketed together?

7. Are the stretchers or rungs original? Do they match each other in shape, color, etc.? If you can see the end of the rung through the leg, it may mean that the rung has been replaced.

8. Has a splint seat been put on a chair that originally had a rush seat? Rush seats leave narrow, closely spaced indentations on the seat rungs. These indentations can be seen by spreading the incorrect splints apart.

9. Are the arms original? Do they match each other in color, wear, etc.? Is there any evidence of new saw cuts or band-saw marks? Is there evidence that the arms have been

moved, e.g., square wood patches in the back posts above the arms?

10. If the chair has finials and/or mushroom handholds, are they right? They should be turned in one piece with the front posts or back posts, respectively.

11. Are the slats, banisters, splat, crest rail, or bottom rail original? For example, do the slats match each other in thickness, bevels, color, etc.? Are the banisters made from the same wood? Sometimes a chair must be taken apart to replace the back parts, which necessitates drilling out the pins on one side. The new pins on that side will then be different in size and shape from the pins on the other side, and they may not fit their holes snugly. Is there any evidence of this?

12. If it is possible to feel or see inside the socket holes, were they made with a pod auger as they should be? That is, do the holes have rounded ends inside?

13. On plank-seat chairs, is the seat made from a single board and does it show jack-plane marks?

14. Does the chair have the tool marks and irregularities of hand manufacture?

15. Does wear appear in logical places, e.g., on the front rungs?

16. Is there any evidence that the chair has been repainted?

17. If there is worm damage, does it appear as pinhead-size holes rather than grooves or channels (except where worn down through use)?

1

1. Carver Chair (1640–1720)

Has a single or double row of three or four turned spindles forming its back. Similar chairs with turned spindles below the seat are called Brewster chairs.

Early Carver chairs are massive, having posts that can be more than 2½ inches in diameter, while later chairs have posts that are less than 2 inches. Sausage turnings are an indication of lateness (about 1710–20). The front posts of armchairs usually end in mushroom handholds. Late Carver chairs were also made as side chairs.

Fig. 1: New England, about 1700. Carver chairs thought to be from northern New Jersey and/or New York are more ornate than the New England chairs, with many closely spaced ball turnings on the front and back posts and vase-and-ball-shaped finials.

Made in all regions, in New England first in ash, then in maple; in New York and New Jersey sometimes in walnut.

Rare. Exp. to v. exp.

2

2. Early Slat-Back Chair (1680–1720)

Is similar in appearance to the Carver chair (fig. 1), but forming its back has three (more rarely four) concave slats that are scrolled, arched, or notched (fig. 2). Some early slat-back chairs have turned spindles below the arms and the seat.

All the slats may be scrolled or arched identically, or the top slat may be more elaborately scrolled than the others. The socketed arms may be flat (fig. 2) or turned. The front and back posts usually have wide ring turnings. The earlier the chair, the more massive are the proportions. Mushroom handholds may be more than 4 inches in diameter. A secondary arm, as in fig. 9, is associated with Connecticut or southeastern Massachusetts.

Fig. 2: New England, about 1710–20. Sausage turnings indicate a date of about 1710 or later. The mushroom handholds, which originated in America about 1690–1700, are always turned in one piece with the front posts. Note especially the heaviness of the ring turnings compared with, for example, fig. 4. This chair has been cut down: the legs are too short and the bottom rungs are missing. Also, the top of the top slat has been broken off.

Made primarily in New England, sometimes in ash, more often in maple with hardwood slats.

Rare. Exp. to v. exp.

3–5. *New England Slat-Back Chair* (*1720–1840*)

Has a back formed from three to five concave slats of various shapes, including arched, scrolled, notched, and serpentine. The slats are sometimes graduated. The top slat is sometimes more elaborately shaped or larger than the others.

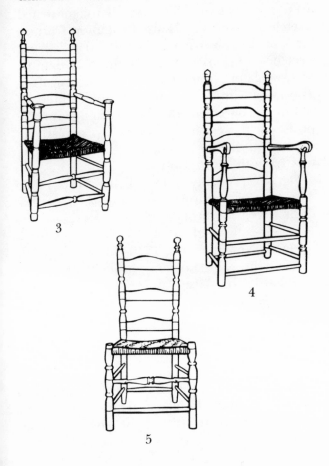

The arms are turned and socketed into the front and back posts (fig. 3), extend over the front posts (fig. 4), or are double bearing (fig. 22). Mushroom handholds (fig. 3) may be over 4 inches in diameter. Sausage-turned stretchers (as in fig. 2) are a common feature. One or two baluster-and-ring turned front stretchers (fig. 5) probably indicate a date of 1730 or later. Double-bearing arms are often associated with Connecticut. As the eighteenth century progressed, the ring turnings on the posts of these chairs became progressively thinner until they disappeared completely, first from the front posts.

Fig. 3: Probably Connecticut, 1740–1800. The tops of the top and second slats of this chair have been broken off.

Fig. 4: New England, 1730–70.

Fig. 5: New England, 1730–50.

Made in New England, usually of maple with hardwood slats.

Numerous. V. inexp. to v. exp.

6. *Roundabout Chair* (*1700–1840*)

Has a low back formed by arms that sweep halfway around the chair. The arms are cut out, as opposed to steam bent, and are joined in the back in various ways but in early chairs almost never simply butt against each other (in fig. 6 there is a lap joint). The applied arm may be nailed in place.

Made over a long time span, these chairs exhibit the stylistic features of their period of manufacture, such as ring turnings, Spanish feet, Queen Anne and Chippendale splats, banister-back combs, Windsor-like spindles, etc. Roundabout chairs are also called corner chairs.

Fig. 6: New England, 1750–1800.

Made in all regions in maple, walnut, and other hard woods.

Not numerous. Mod. exp. to v. exp.

6

7

7, 8. *Delaware Valley Slat-Back Chair* *(1720–1830)*

Has three to six graduated slats that may be arched only on the top (fig. 7), arched on the top and bottom (fig. 8), or, much more rarely, scrolled. The back posts are plain and taper from the seat to the finials. The back feet often taper sharply to the floor. The front feet are almost always ball shaped and wider than the front posts (fig. 7), or blunt-arrow shaped (fig. 8). Finials are often acorn shaped, as in figs. 7 and 8. Armchairs have baluster turnings below the arms and, on the better chairs, ball-and-reel turnings just below the front seat, as on fig. 8. The arms almost always have a cut-

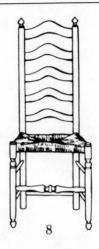

8

out on their undersides, as on fig. 7—a feature found on many Delaware Valley rush- or splint-seat armchairs. Also typical is a single, rarely double, baluster-ring-and-reel turned front stretcher. As the eighteenth century progressed, the posts became thinner, the finials more vertical, the slats fewer in number, and the front stretcher less boldly turned.

Similar chairs associated with northern New Jersey have ring turnings on the posts and urn-shaped finials.

Fig. 7: Probably Pennsylvania, 1740–80.

Fig. 8: Probably Pennsylvania, 1750–1810.

Made in the Delaware Valley, usually in maple with oak or hickory slats.

Fairly numerous. Inexp. to v. exp.

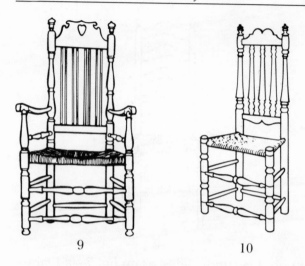

9   10

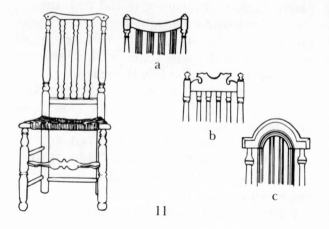

a

b

c

11

9–11. Banister-Back Chair (1700–1830)

Has a back formed by three to six narrow, vertical slats (banisters) mortised into a crest and bottom rail.

The banisters are of two types: turned in a pattern similar to the back posts, split in half lengthwise, and then attached to the chair with their flat sides—or, less commonly, their turned sides—facing forward (figs. 10 and 11); or straight-sided, flat pieces whose front faces are often molded (fig. 9).

Classic, early banister-back chairs from New England have elaborately carved and pierced crest rails in the so-called Prince of Wales pattern and command large sums of money (one recently sold at auction for $11,000). They also have block-and-baluster turnings on the front legs, Spanish feet, block-shaped rear legs that sweep backward, large baluster-and-reel turned front stretchers, and canted backs (similar to fig. 12). The more common chairs have simpler crest rails and ring turnings on the legs. A few banister backs have been found with concave crest and bottom rails. On armchairs, the arms may roll over the front posts, may be socketed into the front posts, or may sweep outward, as in fig. 6. One or two baluster-and-reel turned front stretchers is a typical feature.

Fig. 9: Heart and crown crest rail, New England, probably Connecticut, 1740–1800. Note the secondary arm.

Fig. 10: Double-arch crest rail, New England, 1740–1800.

Fig. 11: Chippendale crest rail, New England, 1760–1800. Note the Chippendale ears at the ends of the crest rail.

Crest rails illustrated: (a) yoke-back, Connecticut, 1710–50; (b) stag-horn or fish-tail, Massachusetts and New Hampshire, 1750–1800; (c) arch-head, Pennsylvania, 1710–30. There are many other styles of crest rails.

Made in all regions in maple and other hard woods.

Fairly numerous. Inexp. to v. exp.

12–15. Queen Anne Chair (1735–1805)

Has a vase-shaped splat, sometimes with ears, with the greatest mass near the top of the splat (as opposed to the nineteenth-century fiddleback chair, as in fig. 21, which places the greatest mass near the bottom).

The classic Queen Anne chair has a spoon-shaped back, like fig. 12; a splat mortised into a shoe attached to the rear seat rail, often with

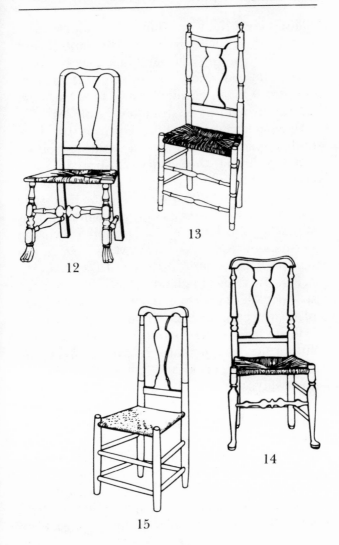

12

13

14

15

nails; a crest rail with rounded shoulders, perhaps with a shell carving in the center; and cabriole legs with claw-and-ball feet or some form of pad foot. More often than not, country Queen Anne chairs have straight backs; turned legs or straight cabriole legs (fig. 14); a baluster-and-reel turned front stretcher; and a splat mortised into a separate bottom rail, as in all the chairs illustrated. Some country chairs do have slip seats, and then the splat is mortised into a shoe as in the high-style chairs; however, some country chairs without slip seats also have a shoe around which the permanent seat must be woven, leaving the seat partially open in the back of the chair.

Fig. 12: New England, 1740–60. Note the spoon back. This chair has the undercarriage of many banister-back chairs of the earlier William and Mary period. Therefore, some authorities might date it earlier than the Queen Anne period and call it "transitional." In reality, the chair probably has a back that has been updated to reflect the latest popular style. The Spanish feet are considered a desirable feature.

Fig. 13: New England, probably Connecticut, 1740–80. This chair has a yoke-shaped crest rail and finials related to Connecticut banister-back chairs from the earlier William and Mary period (similar to fig. a, page 136).

Like fig. 12, it has probably been updated.

Fig. 14: New York, 1740–1805. This chair has straight cabriole legs and pad or club feet that are sometimes called "Dutch" in style. The turned back posts are reminiscent of banister-back chairs.

Fig. 15: Probably New England, 1780–1810. This is a very simple chair.

Made in all regions in such hard woods as maple, walnut, and cherry.

Armchairs are not numerous; side chairs are fairly numerous. Inexp. to v. exp.

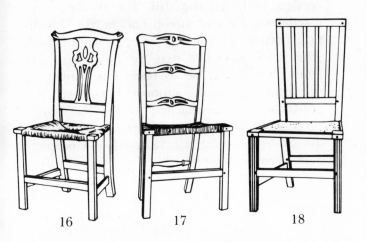

16   17   18

16–18. *Chippendale Chair (1760–1820)*

May have one of several different types of backs, most commonly a pierced splat, sometimes with carved strapwork (fig. 16); pierced or solid horizontal ladders (fig. 17); or a square back with vertical slats (fig. 18). The crest rail usually bows upward in the center, perhaps with a shell carving, and flares outward at the ends, forming ears that may be carved.

Classic Chippendale chairs have cabriole front legs ending in a claw-and-ball foot or some form of pad foot, or square front legs. Most country Chippendale chairs have square, untapered front legs that may be molded, reeded, or fluted (fig. 18). The rear legs are usually square and sweep backward. The inside corners of the legs may be chamfered. The front stretcher may be flush with the front legs or may be set back. On armchairs, the arms are usually supported by posts that penetrate, or are attached to, the seat rungs about halfway between the front and back of the chair, as in fig. 19. (Regarding Chippendale chairs with splats, like fig. 16, see information on the splats of Queen Anne chairs, figs. 12–15.)

Chairs with Chippendale backs may also have undercarriages in the William and Mary style, as in fig. 12.

Fig. 16: Pierced splat, New England, 1760–1810.

Fig. 17: Pierced ladderback, New England, 1760–1810.

Fig. 18: Square back, New England, 1760–1810.

Made in all regions in maple, walnut, and cherry, less frequently in mahogany. Nineteenth-century examples may be made in oak.

Numerous. Inexp. to v. exp.

19

19. *Hepplewhite Chair (1790–1830)*

Usually has a pierced splat with a single reverse curve on each edge (fig. 19) or a late Chippendale-like pierced splat that simply tapers from the top to the bottom. There is usually some design motif in the upper center of the splat, such as the urn in fig. 19. The back posts usually bow out slightly below the crest rail, echoing the general contours of the splat. (Actually, the crest rail and the back posts on fig. 19 down to about where the arms start form the beginnings of a shield-shaped back that is far more characteristic of high-style Hepplewhite chairs than the country versions.) The front legs are square and taper to the floor. The rear legs are square and sweep backward. If stretchers are present, the front stretcher may be flush with the front legs or may be set back. On armchairs, the arms are set back from the front of the chair. The arm supports penetrate or are attached to the seat rungs or rails and may also be attached to the side stretchers. (Regarding the attachment of the splat, see information on the splats of Queen Anne chairs, figs. 12–15.)

A great many country Hepplewhite chairs borrow such Chippendale design features as ears at the ends of the crest rail and square, untapered legs.

Fig. 19: New England, 1790–1815.

Made in all regions of various hard woods, including oak.

Not numerous. Mod. exp. to exp.

20

20. Hitchcock, or Fancy, Chair (1800–1840)

Has turned "Sheraton" legs that may be splayed, bent, or straight. The backs are made in various designs, including a broad slat (fig. 20), a slat with such cutout patterns as an eagle or "turtle," flattened spindles, and narrowly spaced horizontal rods with balls between them. The seats may be rush, cane, or plank. On armchairs, the arms are usually scrolled at the ends and are supported by turned spindles attached to the seat.

The earliest chairs are hand decorated and may have seats that are rounded in front

(1800–1820). From about 1820 on, these chairs were stencil decorated and mass produced in factories by the thousands.

Generically, all similar fancy chairs are called Hitchcock chairs after the famous Connecticut mass-producer of them. Chairs actually made in one of Lambert Hitchcock's factories may be labeled in stencil on the back edge of the seat. From about 1825 to 1829, the chairs were marked "L. HITCHCOCK. HITCH-COCKS-VILLE. CONN. WARRANTED."; from about 1829 to 1843, "HITCHCOCK. ALFORD. & CO. HITCHCOCKS-VILLE. CONN. WARRANTED."; from about 1843 to 1852, "LAMBERT HITCHCOCK. UNIONVILLE. CONN."

Fig. 20: Hitchcock chair, Connecticut, about 1835.

Made in all regions, usually in maple.

Common. Inexp. to mod. exp.

21. Fancy Chair, Pennsylvania Type (1820–60)

Has a scrolled crest rail (fig. 21) or the so-called balloon back (vaguely resembling a bow-back Windsor chair, fig. 30) with some variation of a fiddleback splat. The seat is a single plank of wood, and the legs are ring or bamboo turned.

These chairs were hand decorated or stenciled and *must* carry their original paint to be worth buying. They were made in sets of up to twelve chairs, sometimes with a single rocking chair. Similar chairs made in the Victorian era have seats made of more than one piece of wood; in addition, the back posts may be made of more than one piece of wood.

Fig. 21: Pennsylvania region, 1820–60. This form of back is often called a bootjack splat.

Made in all regions, but primarily in or near Pennsylvania, usually of maple.

Common. V. inexp. to inexp.

21

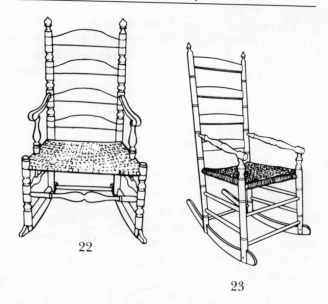

22

23

22, 23. *Slat-Back Rocking Chair*
(1780–1840)

Is essentially similar to rockerless slat-back
chairs and exhibits the style characteristics of
the period in which it was made.

True eighteenth-century rocking chairs are
fairly rare, since rocking did not become a national pastime until the nineteenth century.
The rockers on eighteenth-century chairs extend approximately the same distance from
the front and rear legs of the chair, are taller
than they are wide, and are mortised and

pinned into the legs (fig. 22). On nineteenth-century chairs, the rockers become longer in the rear than in the front, adding stability and comfort. In addition, after about 1825 the practice began of socketing the legs into the rockers rather than mortising the rockers into the legs.

Apparently the rocking chair is an American invention that evolved from the rockers on cradles. Rockers that are taller than they are wide go by various colorful names, such as carpet cutters, ankle skinners, and cheese cutters. Generally speaking, rocking chairs with arms are far more desirable than those without them.

Fig. 22: New England, probably Connecticut, 1780–1800. Note the double-bearing arms, which have led these chairs to be called hoop-skirt rocking chairs because they give a wider berth to a woman's full skirt.

Fig. 23: Possibly New Jersey, 1810–30. Interestingly, the arms on this chair appear to slant downward but are actually parallel to the floor when no one is sitting in the chair. Note the turnings on the arms, which resemble the legs of many Sheraton tables, such as fig. 84.

Made in all regions in various hard woods, usually maple.

Common in their nineteenth-century varieties. Inexp. to exp.

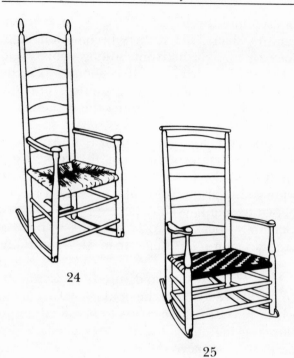

24

25

24, 25. *Shaker Slat-Back Rocking Chair* (1820–1930)

Has three to five arched slats and plain posts except for turnings under the arms of armchairs. The back posts may end in simple finials (fig. 24) or in a cushion rail (fig. 25). The arms may be socketed into the front posts (fig.

24), may roll over the front posts, may curve outward from the front posts, or may sit atop the front posts (fig. 23). The rockers are mortised into the legs; on late chairs they may be screwed or nailed in place rather than pinned. In chairs like fig. 24, the mushroom handhold is turned in one piece with the front posts; in chairs like fig. 23, the button handholds are a separate piece doweled into the front posts through the arms. The seats may be rush, splint, or fabric tape (fig. 25; the Shakers made this tape in fourteen different colors ranging from black to grass green to orange). Some chairs have fabric tape on the back rather than slats.

After 1873, some chairs that were mass produced at Mount Lebanon, New York, for "the World" have gold identifying decals on the inside of one of the rockers or on the back of a slat that read, "SHAKER'S / NO. [here the model number, or size, ranging from 0 to 7 was included] / TRADE MARK / MT. LEBANON, N.Y." There was also a small drawing of a rocking chair.

Side chairs and armchairs without rockers are similar in appearance to the rocking chairs. The Shakers made chairs in a wide variety of styles in different communities; at Mount Lebanon alone more than fifty different models were produced. The Mount Lebanon and Watervliet, New York, chairs are perhaps the best known.

Fig. 24: Watervliet, New York, 1820–70.

Fig. 25: Mount Lebanon, New York, 1835– early twentieth century.

Almost always made in maple.

Fairly common. Inexp. to exp.

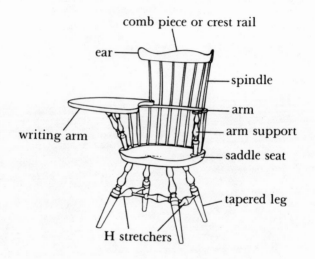

comb piece or crest rail

ear

writing arm

spindle

arm

arm support

saddle seat

tapered leg

H stretchers

WINDSOR AND WINDSOR-DERIVED CHAIRS
7

CONSTRUCTION

Legs, stretchers, and arm supports. These parts are turned, except for ram's horn arm supports (fig. 31), which are sawed. They are usually made of maple, although such woods as oak, beech, and hickory are also found. The stretchers are socketed into each other and into the legs, where they may be pinned or blind wedged. The legs are socketed into the seat—more often than not penetrating it—and are wedged. Chairs with hardwood seats are the most likely to have legs that do not penetrate but are held with blind wedges. The arm supports penetrate the seat and are wedged. They may or may not penetrate the arms. If they do, they are wedged; if they don't, they are usually pinned or blind wedged. On probably nine out of ten Windsor armchairs, the turning pattern of the arm supports echoes that of the legs.

Seat. The seat is made of a single board about 2 inches thick that, on the better chairs, is chamfered on the edges and may be dished out in its center to half its thickness. Furthermore, a curved line about ⅛ to ¼ inch wide is usually chiseled out of the seat around all the parts that enter the seat from above; the line may also extend around the back edge of the seat. The wood used is usually relatively soft, such as pine, poplar, or chestnut, but seats of maple and other hard woods are found, especially if the entire chair is made of that same wood. On brace-back chairs, the tailpiece may be separately mortised and pinned in place, but only if the grain runs across the seat rather than from front to back, for example, in an oval seat as opposed to a shield-shaped one. A few Windsor chairs are known with seats originally upholstered in leather. Also, I have been told that some early Windsors do have seats made of more than one piece of wood, but I have never seen one and would probably be suspicious of it.

Spindles. No matter how many parts of the chair the spindles pass through, they are always single pieces of wood, turned or spoke shaved and made of a springy wood such as hickory. Where springiness is unimportant, as on a low-back chair, they may be made of maple. They do not penetrate the seat. Except for Rhode Island low-back chairs and the applied arms of Pennsylvania low-back chairs, some, and usually all, of the spindles penetrate the arms and the bow, where they are wedged or pinned.

Arms. On low-back chairs, fanback and bow-back armchairs, and comb-back chairs with applied arms, the arms are shaped by sawing. Those on other types of Windsors are steam bent. Steam-bent arms are usually made of oak or hickory. Sawed arms may be made of those woods or of other hard woods such as maple or, more rarely, unpainted walnut or mahogany. Knuckle or scrolled handholds may be one piece or two piece. If the latter, the applied pieces are attached from the side and/or from below and are usually pinned.

Bow. This is usually made of oak, hickory, or ash and steam bent. It penetrates the part to which it is attached (i.e., the arm or seat) and is wedged.

Comb piece. This is usually made of steam-bent oak and is almost always pinned in the back through the spindles in at least two places.

EXAMINATION CHECKLIST

(Note: Many of the items to be checked on Windsor chairs are the same as for chairs in general, Chapter 6. The following are additional items that apply specifically to Windsors.)

1. Is the seat one piece of wood about 2 inches thick in its thickest part? Does the seat have shallow gouges running with the grain on its bottom, indicating that it was hand smoothed with a jack plane? Is there any evidence of new saw cuts along the outer edges of the seat, an indication that it may have been made up from a settee seat? If there is an ornamental chisel line on the top of the seat toward the back, does it surround all the parts that enter the seat from above, including the arm supports? If not, a side chair has been converted to an armchair. Is there any evidence of new planing to reshape the seat and make it "better" (more dished out or chamfered)?

2. Does the chair show signs of shrinkage with age? This is especially prominent in many old Windsors where the spindles penetrate various parts. For example, the spindles tend to protrude through the crest rail or, if their upper ends are held firmly, they may bow outward.

3. Have the legs been pieced out? This is often, but not always, done on Windsors where there are ring turnings on the legs. If the chair is stripped, are the legs the same

color as each other? Is each leg the same color (and, for that matter, the same wood) above and below the ring turnings?

4. Are the spindles original? Do they match each other in turnings and texture? Is there a sudden bend to the right or left in a spindle above where it passes through a part of the chair, which is not present in most of the other spindles? If so, the spindle with the bend may be new. If the spindles pass through a chair part and continue upward, try twisting them to determine if they are made of one piece of wood, as they should be. Check the tops of the spindles where they are wedged to see if the workmanship looks the same on all of them or appears to be new on any of them.

5. Are the arm supports the same in texture and turnings? Upend the chair and look at where the arm supports penetrate the seat. Are there any new saw cuts at the end of the arm supports, new wedges, or extra holes indicating that the arm supports may have been replaced?

6. Check the bow or back posts for the same items as number 5. Some chairs may have had their entire crest rail replaced.

7. If the legs penetrate the seat, do the tops of the legs seem almost as worn as the rest of the seat around them? (Because the legs are almost always a harder wood than the seat, they

will not show quite as much wear; however, there should be some evidence of wear.)

8. On chairs with knuckle handholds, does the carving on the knuckles look as old as the handwork on the rest of the chair? If not, perhaps the knuckles have been newly carved on plain handholds.

9. On comb-back and fanback Windsors, is there any evidence that the comb piece is new or that its ears have been newly carved to make them "better"?

10. Old Windsors were invariably painted, most frequently green or black but also red, yellow, or white. Even on stripped chairs, traces of old paint usually remain in places where the parts join, in narrow turnings, on the bottom of the seat, and in the wide grains of the oak, hickory, or ash parts. Is there evidence that the parts have the same paint history?

26, 27. *Low-Back Windsor Chair* *(1750–1800)*

Has a back formed by flattened arms about ¾ to ⅞ inch thick that curve outward at the ends, an applied arm at the rear, and short spindles of the same length. The arm supports are placed at the front corners of the seat. The seat is large and D-shaped.

Low-back Windsors are basically Pennsylvania or Rhode Island types. On the Pennsylvania chairs, the arm supports and spindles penetrate the flattened arms but not the applied arm at the rear of the chair. The applied arm has a concave indentation running around its back. The flattened arms meet the applied arm in a lap joint. The spindles are not ornamentally turned. The seat is squared off at the front corners.

On the Rhode Island chairs, the arm supports and spindles do not penetrate either the flattened arms or the applied arm. The ap-

26   27

plied arm is flat in the back. The flattened arms meet each other in a butt joint at the rear of the chair, and the applied arm sits on top of them. The spindles are ornamentally turned. The seat flares out at the front corners, and this motif is echoed in tiny carved points on the outside edge of the flattened arms where the handholds begin. Also, many Rhode Island low-back Windsors have ornamentally turned X-stretchers.

Fig. 26: Pennsylvania, 1750–70. Many authorities have said that the Pennsylvania low-back Windsor chair is the earliest form of Windsor in the American style, and that the Pennsylvania comb-back Windsor, like fig. 28, evolved from it. However, there is no direct or indirect evidence to support this conclusion, and the two forms probably evolved simultaneously. See also comments on fig. 28.

Fig. 27: Rhode Island, 1760–90.

Made in Pennsylvania, Rhode Island, and probably New York City (Pennsylvania style) in a combination of hard and soft woods. Some Rhode Island chairs are made entirely in a hard wood such as maple.

Rare. V. exp.

(Note: The low-back style was revived in the mid-nineteenth century in a form usually called a firehouse Windsor or captain's chair, which is almost always factory made.)

28

28. *Comb-Back Windsor Chair*
(1750–1820)

Has a back resembling a comb, which is formed by a continuation of the spindles through the arms, ending in a comb piece. The arms may be a single steam-bent piece of wood (fig. 28) or they may break in the rear and have an applied arm on top, as in figs. 26 and 27.

Fig. 28: Philadelphia, 1750–70. The cylindrical leg that ends in a blunt arrow or a ball is a typical Pennsylvania feature. This form of leg was largely abandoned about 1770 for a tapered leg, as in fig. 32. Another feature of early Pennsylvania comb-backs and low-backs (fig. 26) is that the medial stretcher is located toward the rear of the side stretchers rather than in their center.

See also fig. 34, another comb-back Windsor.

Made in all regions in a combination of hard and soft woods. Occasionally found in a single hard wood.

Not numerous. Exp. to v. exp.

29

29. *Fanback Windsor Chair (1755–1830)*

Has a back formed by spindles that fan outward up to a crest rail, or comb piece.

On armchairs, the arms are mortised through the back posts and are usually supported by two extra spindles on each side in addition to the arm supports. Fanback Windsors were also made with braced backs, as in fig. 33.

Fig. 29: Probably New England, 1770–1800.

Made in all regions from a combination of hard and soft woods.

Numerous as side chairs; fairly rare as armchairs. Inexp. to v. exp.

30   31

30, 31. Bow-Back Windsor Chair (1760–1840)

Has a back formed by a continuous steam-bent bow that is wedged into the seat.

On armchairs, the arms are usually mortised through the bow. Bow-back Windsors were also made with braced backs, as in fig. 33. These chairs are sometimes called loop-back Windsors.

Fig. 30: Lisbon, Connecticut, 1764–1803. This chair, made by Connecticut craftsman Ebenezer Tracy, can be dated fairly accurately, since the dates of Tracy's working life are known. Note the long taper of the legs compared with the Pennsylvania Windsor, fig. 32, and the sharply chamfered edges of the seat.

Fig. 31: Pennsylvania, 1800–1830. Bamboo turnings were popular on Windsor furniture after about 1800, but most chairs do not have the boldness of fig. 31 or the excellent saddle seat. The ram's horn arm supports and long serpentine arms are a typical Pennsylvania feature.

Made in all regions in a combination of hard and soft woods.

Fairly common as a side chair; not numerous as an armchair. Inexp. to v. exp.

32. *Sack-Back Windsor Chair* (*1765–1840*)

Has a back formed by a bowed crest rail that is mortised and wedged into curved arms and spindles that extend through the arms up to the crest rail. The arms are almost always a single piece of steam-bent wood, but some chairs are known with applied arms in the rear, like fig. 26. Some chairs also have a short comblike extension in the back of three to seven of the central spindles, which end in a comb piece. Sack-back Windsors invariably have oval seats.

In early inventories and advertisements the term "sack-back" appears, but no one knows for certain what type of Windsor chair it refers to. Some authorities believe that it was this type of Windsor, since a sack could obviously be tied to the back of the chair to protect the sitter from drafts.

Fig. 32: Philadelphia, 1765–90. Note the short, thick tapering legs characteristic of Pennsylvania chairs in comparison with fig. 30.

32

Made in all regions in a combination of hard and soft woods.

Numerous. Mod. exp. to v. exp.

33

33. *Continuous-Arm Windsor Chair* *(1760–1830)*

Has a back and arms that are formed by one continuous piece of steam-bent wood.

These chairs have an inherent structural weakness at the point where the arms bend upward to form the back. They are often found with repairs or replacements at that point.

Fig. 33: Lisbon, Connecticut, 1764–1803. (This is an Ebenezer Tracy chair; see comments on fig. 30.) Note the V-shaped braces on the back that help to support the crest rail and add visual interest.

Made in New England and New York in a combination of hard and soft woods.

Not numerous. Mod. exp. to v. exp.

34   35

34, 35. *Writing Arm Windsor Chair* (1755–1840)

Has a flat, paddlelike piece of wood that forms the right arm, which may be attached to another arm beneath it. The writing arm is held by up to three arm supports that are often socketed into one or two side extensions of the seat. These chairs may also have one or two drawers and/or a candle slide beneath the writing arm and another drawer under the seat.

Writing armchairs were made in all the Windsor styles. On comb-back writing armchairs, the comb is sometimes offset slightly to the left of center of the chair.

Fig. 34: Connecticut, 1760–1800. This is a comb-back Windsor; see also fig. 28.

Fig. 35: Possibly New England, 1800–1830. This is a good example of a bamboo-turned Windsor in the Sheraton style, sometimes called a rod-back or a butterfly-back because of the supposed butterfly-shaped medallion below the top rail. Similar chairs whose arms and arm supports form a point are called duckbill armchairs. Note how the stretchers have lost the characteristic H-pattern of earlier Windsors.

Made in all regions in a combination of hard and soft woods.

Fairly rare. Exp. to v. exp.

36, 37. Rod-Back Windsor Chair (1800–1840)

Has a back formed by spindles that may or may not curve backward and may be bamboo turned. The crest rails are usually simple. The legs may be bamboo turned or may simply have shallow, incised rings.

Fig. 36: Step-down Windsor, possibly Pennsylvania region, 1820–40.

Fig. 37: Thumb-back Windsor, possibly New England, 1820–40. The flattened tops of the back posts supposedly resemble thumbs. These chairs are also called rabbit-ear Windsors, for obvious reasons.

Made in all regions in a combination of hard and soft woods, or sometimes entirely in a hard wood such as maple.

Common. V. inexp. to inexp.

36

37

38

38. *Arrow-Back Chair (1810–40)*

Has a back formed by flattened spindles that are shaped like arrows. On armchairs, there may be arrow spindles between the arms and the seat.

This style may have originated in Pennsylvania.

Fig. 38: Possibly Pennsylvania, 1810–30. This rocking chair has a writing arm, a fairly rare feature. Arrow-back side chairs basically resemble figs. 36 and 37.

Made in all regions in a combination of hard

and soft woods or sometimes entirely in a hard wood such as maple.

Common. V. inexp. to mod. exp.

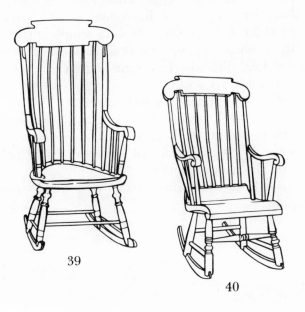

39

40

39, 40. *Salem Rocker (1815–30) and Boston Rocker (1820–40)*

Have backs formed by long spindles that curve backward and then forward. The Salem rocker has a plank seat that is chamfered on the edges. The somewhat later Boston rocker has a rolled seat made from three pieces of wood. On late Boston rockers, the legs are socketed into the rockers.

Both of these chairs were almost always paint decorated. Their crest rails, as shown here, are believed to have been in style prior to 1835. Later crest rails were simplified to a shape with no projections on the top and with end lobes that are flat on the bottom where the rear posts are socketed.

Fig. 39: Probably New England, 1815–30.

Fig. 40: Probably New England, 1820–35. Many Boston rockers were mass produced, some in the factories of Lambert Hitchcock (see Hitchcock chair, fig. 20).

Made in all regions, usually of maple and pine.

Common. Inexp. to mod. exp.

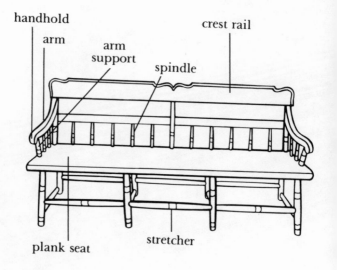

handhold

arm

arm support

spindle

crest rail

plank seat

stretcher

SETTLES, SETTEES,
AND BENCHES
8

CONSTRUCTION

Settles. In unpaneled settles, the backboards meet each other in some form of joint—tongue and groove, lap, spline, or butt—and are nailed in place. They may or may not be random width. Usually there is one or more bracing boards running transversely across the backboards, especially in settles with curved backs; there may also be a bracing board across the top front of the backboards. The sides are made of single boards 15 inches or more in width. The seat is rabbeted into the sides and may be nailed. Diagonal braces may run from the bottom front edge of the seat to the lower back. If there is a vertical board below the seat—usually the front side of a hutch storage compartment—it is often attached to the sides with large open dovetails, and the seat is hinged for access to the hutch.

In paneled settles, the stiles and rails are

mortised and pinned. The panels are usually, but not always, raised. On flat panels, there is often applied molding attached with brads. When the arms are separate pieces, they are mortised and pinned into the back posts and usually roll over the front posts, where they are wedged or pinned.

Benches. These have single-board seats. The legs usually penetrate the seat through two square open mortises and are wedged. There is almost always some sort of stretcher connecting the legs or angled side braces connecting the legs to the seat. On benches with drawers beneath the seat, the board beneath the drawers acts as a stretcher.

Settees. These pieces are constructed in the same way as chairs are. See construction notes on chairs, p. 123, and on Windsor chairs, p. 155.

Drawers. If the piece has drawers, see construction information for chests of drawers, p. 237.

EXAMINATION CHECKLIST

Unpaneled Settles
1. Are the backboards original? Do they match each other in color and textural quality? Do they have the shallow gouges left by a jack

plane or parallel kerf marks left by a pit saw? No circular saw marks should be found.

2. Are the nails used in construction old, i.e., rose head or square head? Does the wood around them seem to have shrunk, indicating that they have been in place for quite a while?

3. Are the sides made from single boards?

4. Check under the seat: is the color of the wood the same under the seat and inside the legs?

5. Do the bottoms of the feet and the bottoms of the backboards, if they extend to the floor, show the proper dotage?

6. If the settle was originally painted, do all the parts show the same paint history?

7. Is the evidence of wear logical? For example, if there are scrolled arms, are the tops and curves worn where the sitters' arms would come in contact with them?

8. Is there any evidence of new band-saw marks, which look like narrow grooves along, and perpendicular to, the edges of the boards?

9. If the settle has drawers, see the examination checklist for chests of drawers, p. 241, item number 2.

Paneled Settles

1. Are the panels hand chamfered or smoothed, both front and back? Do they

match each other in style and quality of work-manship?

2. Are the stiles and rails pinned in place?

3. If there are separate arms, are they pinned or wedged in place? Are they worn logically?

4. If there are stretchers, are they mortised and pinned into the legs? Do they show logical wear, i.e., are the front stretchers more worn than the side or rear stretchers?

5. Does any molding show the irregularities of handwork? Is applied molding attached with square brads or perhaps pins?

6. If the settle has separate legs and feet, have they been pieced out? Do the feet show the proper dotage?

7. If the settle has drawers, see the examination checklist for chests of drawers, p. 241, item number 2.

Benches

See the applicable items under *Settles,* above.

Settees

See the examination checklist for chairs, p. 125, or Windsor and Windsor-derived chairs, p. 157—whichever applies to the form of the piece.

41

41. Settle (1700–1840)

Has a high back, presumably to protect sitters from drafts, which may be paneled or made from plain boards (fig. 41).

Settles may be found with such refinements as curved backs (fig. 41), canopies, scrolled arms, drawers beneath the seat, shelves built into the back, center armrests, and hutches. They are one of the most difficult forms to date with any accuracy. Settles with paneled backs seem to have been made as late as 1800, long after wainscot (paneled) chairs went out of fashion in the early eighteenth century. Un-paneled settles with uniform-width boards in the back are nineteenth century. An examination of the nails used in construction might help in dating

Fig. 41: Probably New England, late eighteenth or early nineteenth century. Settles with curved backs, as here, are often called barrel-back settles.

Made in all regions, primarily in pine.

Not numerous. Mod. exp. to v. exp.

42. *Settle Bed, or* Banc-Lit *(1750–1840)*

Resembles a settle with a low back, but the bottom structure is a box that converts into a bed.

Most settle beds work on the principle of fig. 42: the front boards are hinged at the bottom, allowing the seat to swing out to form an open sleeping box (the seat becomes the front side of the box, the front boards become the bottom). Other settle beds simply have a person-

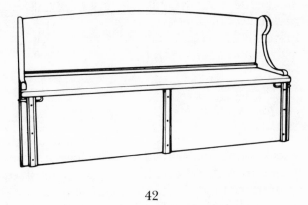

42

size drawer in the bottom that can be pulled out to form the sleeping box.

Settle beds are a Canadian form that may have originated in Ireland. However, they were probably made and used in northern New England.

Fig. 42: New England or Canada, 1750–1820.

Made in New England and Canada, the simpler pieces in pine, the more elaborate ones in various hard woods.

Not numerous. Mod. exp. to v. exp.

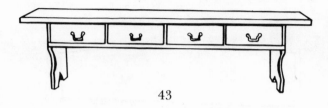

43

43. Bench (1640–1840)

Generally has legs formed from single boards with cutouts for feet. The legs are connected to each other with a stretcher or skirt, or they are braced into the plank seat.

Pennsylvania benches often have scrolled legs; the rear legs are often left flat so that the bench can be used close to a wall, as in fig. 43.

Fig. 43: Probably Pennsylvania, 1760–1820. Most benches, except for their old paint or scrolled legs, are not stylistically very inspiring. This one, with its lipped drawers, is well above average.

Made in all regions, usually in pine.

Common. Inexp. to mod. exp.

(Note: Sometimes butcher, or slaughter, benches are cut down to sitting height and sold as benches. They can be recognized by their peg legs and very thick plank "seats," which naturally are deeply scarred from the butcher's cleaver and knives.)

44

44. *Wagon Seat (1750–1840)*

Resembles two small side-by-side armchairs.

Wagon seats were made in a variety of chair styles ranging from eighteenth-century slat back to nineteenth-century arrow back. In the slat-back form, there are usually only two slats. They were probably made to be removable from the wagon and also made in sets. Sometimes the outside edges of the legs are worn or flattened from their snug fit inside the wagon, as in fig. 44.

Fig. 44: New England, 1800–1840. Note how the center legs are thicker than the others to accommodate a double seat rung over which the splint seat has been woven.

Made primarily in southern New England and the Middle Atlantic region in maple and other hard woods.

Not numerous. Mod. exp. to exp.

45, 46. Settee (1730–1840)

Has the basic form of the armchairs of the period in which it was made. Settees usually have plank seats, occasionally rush or splint seats.

For dating, compare with the chairs of various periods. Nineteenth-century pieces are frequently paint decorated.

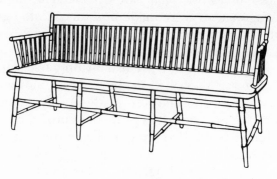

45

Fig. 45: Possibly New England, 1800–1830. Compare this piece with fig. 33.

Fig. 46: Pennsylvania or New Jersey, 1820–40. This piece has what is called a half-spindle back, a Windsor-derived style. Note the way the large scrolled arms swoop up to meet the crest rail, which is typical of Pennsylvania and New Jersey pieces. Also, compare the crest rail with that of fig. 21.

Made in all regions, usually in a combination of hard and soft woods.

Fairly common, but rare in early Windsor forms.

Mod. exp. to v. exp.

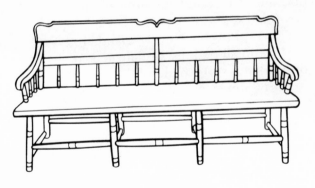

46

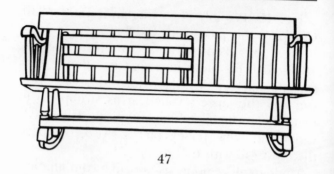

47

47. *Mammy Bench, or Rocking Settee (1820–40)*

Resembles a small settee but has rockers and a removable gate that was used as a cradle.

Mammy benches are a relatively late invention and are found in the rod-back (fig. 47), arrow-back, and fancy-chair styles.

Fig. 47: Possibly New England, 1820–40.

Made in all regions, usually in a combination of hard and soft woods.

Fairly numerous. Mod. exp. to exp.

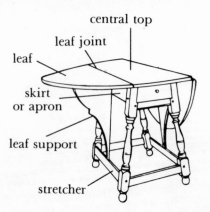

central top

leaf joint

leaf

skirt
or apron

leaf support

stretcher

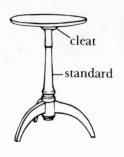

cleat

standard

TABLES AND STANDS
9

CONSTRUCTION

Tops and leaves. Tops may be multiple- or single-board. Multiple-board tops tend to have boards that are connected with some sort of interlocking or overlapping joint to compensate for shrinkage, which otherwise would cause gaps between them. Also, adjoining boards are usually positioned with their end grains facing in different directions; thus, if adjoining boards warped, they would warp in opposite directions, which would have the effect of keeping them flat.

Permanently attached tops are held fast in several ways. On many early tables, there are pins hammered through the top from above into the tops of the legs or the cleat. Other methods include nails or screws inserted through the top from above; nails or screws inserted through a cleat; or nails or screws inserted at an angle through the inner edge of the apron from below (the spot where the screw goes through the apron is usually chiseled out).

Removable tops are held in place with short, slide-out pins or long rods that go through transverse cleats under the top and through the table's skirt. The cleats sometimes slide into dovetail slots or rabbets cut into the underside of the top.

Breadboard ends on tops or leaves may simply be nailed in place. In more sophisticated construction, they are held with tongue-and-groove or mortise-and-tenon joints that are pinned from the edges or through the tops of the breadboard ends.

Leaves are connected to the central top with a variety of hinges, the most common being the wrought- or cast-iron butt hinge but also including butterfly hinges and cotter-pin hinges. Card tables often have special brass hinges on the edges of their leaves. Butt hinges are usually set into chiseled-out cuts in the underside of the top and leaves. Hinges are attached with screws or with nails that may be clinched back through the top.

Leaves are almost always single boards that are frequently found warped. In the simplest tables, the leaves meet the central top in a butt joint (fig. 85). In early tables, up to about 1725, there is a tongue-and-groove joint (fig. 56); later tables have a rule joint, which looks like a quarter-round molding at the edge of the central top that fits into a quarter-round cut in the leaf (fig. 73).

Apron. Until the nineteenth century, aprons were attached to the legs with pinned mortise-and-tenon joints. In nineteenth-century construction, the apron may slide into dovetail slots cut into the leg from the top and may be glued in place. Open dovetailing of the apron into the legs is extremely rare.

Legs. The legs are turned or shaped from a single piece of wood, except for some trestle tables.

Stretchers. These may be turned, square, or horizontally or vertically flat. They are attached to the legs with pinned mortise-and-tenon joints, although in the nineteenth century they may be glued. In American construction, stretchers are usually, but not always, set flush with the outer faces of the legs.

Drawers. Drawers are either set into a cutout in the apron or into a framework made of separate pieces of wood. On some unlipped table drawers, the sides project beyond the back of the drawer and act as a stop. For more information, see chests of drawers, p. 237.

EXAMINATION CHECKLIST

1. Is the top original? The following items may indicate a replaced top: different paint history from the rest of the table; holes that seem to serve no purpose; difference in color between the underside of the top and the inside of the skirt, especially if the top and apron are made of the same wood; refinishing of the underside of the top and the inside of the skirt to make them appear to be the same color; wear and/or stains on the underside of the top within the boundaries of the skirt (however, the top *should* be worn on its underside beyond the boundaries of the skirt—i.e., where it overhangs—where, for example, people may have struck matches; but see note below); top boards that do not match in color; new saw cuts; lack of wear on the edges of the top; evidence of a shadow mark from another table; and no indication of hand planing (hand planing is more evident in softwood tops than in hardwood ones). If necessary, you may wish to pry up the top slightly to see if the nail, screw, or pin holes through it match those in the skirt or cleat. (Note: A. On some country tables the top may in fact be original but may

be worn on the underside because it was reversed years ago so that the less worn side would be uppermost; B. Parallel saw cuts are sometimes made on the underside of tops by restorers to help straighten serious warpage; C. Occasionally a stand is found whose "original" top was actually made from a cutting board, so the underside may be excessively worn.)

2. Are the leaves original? Do the joints where the top and the leaves meet look handmade? Are the leaves single boards (they usually are)? Do the planing marks on the leaves feel like those on the central top? Is the color on the underside of the leaves the same as that on the underside of the central top, especially where they meet? Are the hinge cutouts and holes for nails or screws the same on the leaves and the central top? Are there wear marks under the leaves caused by contact from whatever mechanism supports the leaves?

3. Has the table been cut down, or have the legs been pieced out? Do the feet show the proper dotage? Are the pins attaching the legs to the apron and the stretchers to the legs slightly projecting and polygonal? Do the pins fit their holes snugly? Are turned legs slightly out of round? Are there scribe marks on the inside of the tops of the legs marking the

limits of the mortise into which the apron fits, an indication of handwork?

4. If the table has stretchers, are they worn logically? For example, in tables with drawers, the side of the table opposite the drawers was often pushed against a wall; thus the stretcher on that side would be worn less than the stretcher beneath the drawer.

5. Regarding drawers, see the examination checklist for chest of drawers, p. 241, item 2.

48, 49. Trestle Table (1650–1840)

Has a base composed of two or three trestles—vertical columns ending in some sort of foot and topped by transverse supports on which the tabletop rests. The trestles themselves are linked by a long stretcher. There may also be extra braces, as in fig. 49.

A true trestle table is not permanently joined but can be dismantled for storage by the removal of the pegs or key wedges that hold it together. Seventeenth-century trestle tables are as much as 12 feet long and have single-board pine tops 22 to 30 inches wide and chamfered oak trestles. Later tables are usually shorter and have multiple-board tops, often with breadboard ends. Some Shaker

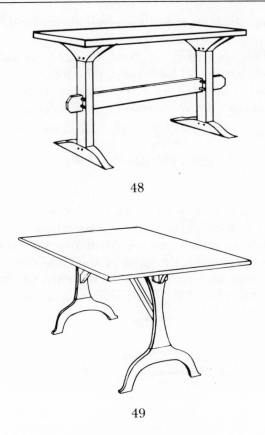

48

49

trestle tables have transverse cleats below the top.

Fig. 48: New England, seventeenth or early eighteenth century.

Fig. 49: Harvard, Massachusetts, nineteenth century. This is a Shaker trestle table.

Made primarily in New England, usually with a hardwood base and a pine top.

Early examples are extremely rare. Later examples are not numerous. Exp. to v. exp.

50, 51. Tavern Table (1660–1840)

Typically designates a relatively small table with up to two drawers, a rectangular top, and turned legs connected by stretchers. The stretchers, which may be turned or flat, may be set higher on the sides of the table than in the front and rear. Breadboard ends on the top and splayed legs are common features.

50

Many small tables are called tavern tables. Some of the variants include round or polygonal tops; one or two drop leaves; three legs; square tapered legs (after 1790); and cabriole legs not connected by stretchers. Tavern tables with removable tops are associated with Pennsylvania, as are tables with drawers of different widths (see figs. 54 and 55).

Fig. 50: New England, 1720–1800. This table has the most typical New England leg turning pattern.

Fig. 51: Probably Pennsylvania, 1720–60. Turned medial stretchers are often associated with Pennsylvania and Southern tavern tables.

Made in all regions, often with walnut, maple, or cherry bases and pine tops.

Fairly numerous. Mod. exp. to v. exp.

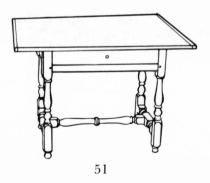

51

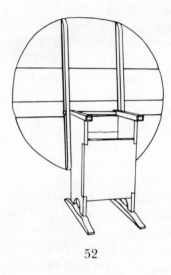

52

52, 53. *Chair Table* (1660–1840)

Has a base that resembles a chair, usually with arms. The top is typically round, and its boards are held together by two cleats attached to the chair base with pins or a long rod, allowing the top to swing up and down.

Stylistic variations include square tops, turned arms and legs, stretchers, drawers, and hutches.

Note that on both tables illustrated, the cleats extend all the way to the edge of the tops. Thus you should expect to find the top

53

worn on either side of each cleat but hardly worn at all very close to where the cleats are attached.

Fig. 52: Probably New England, eighteenth century. Note the shoe feet on this table, which are usually considered a desirable feature and an indication of eighteenth-century construction.

Fig. 53: Possibly New England, nineteenth century.

Made in all regions, often entirely in soft wood.

Fairly numerous. Mod. exp. to v. exp.

54

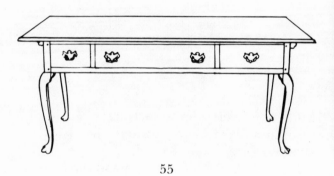

55

54, 55. *Library Table (1660–1840)*

Is essentially a large version of a tavern table (see figs. 50 and 51).

Fig. 54: Pennsylvania, 1720–60. Drawers of unequal widths are associated with Pennsylvania, as is this type of flat stretcher.

Fig. 55: Pennsylvania, 1755–95. Trifid feet are often associated with Pennsylvania. Note, too, that the tops of both of these pieces are removable, another Pennsylvania feature.

Made in all regions with hardwood bases and hardwood or softwood tops.

Not numerous. V. exp.

56

56. Gateleg Table (1670–1840)

Typically has six or eight turned legs connected by turned stretchers. Resembling a gate in form, one leg on each side swings out to support the leaves. The gate legs are hinged with dowels cut directly into their ends, which fit into holes drilled in the apron and the stretchers. When the gate legs are closed, they fit flush into cutouts in the apron and stretcher. The top is usually oval or, less often, rectangular. There may be a drawer in one or both ends.

Some of the large eight-legged tables have two gate legs on each side that are hinged near the corners of the apron and ends of the stretchers.

Variations include: a single drop leaf; turned stationary legs but square gate legs; all square legs; vertically split gate legs (rare); and two centrally pivoting gate legs that support a tilt top (the so-called tuckaway table, another rare form).

Fig. 56: New England, 1700–1740.

Made in all regions, usually in a solid hard wood such as walnut, maple, or cherry. Some tables have pine tops; some are entirely pine, and they usually have unturned legs.

Not numerous. Exp. to v. exp.

57, 58. Sawbuck Table (1670–1840)

Has a rectangular top that rests on, or is attached to, X-shaped legs connected by a long stretcher. Where the legs cross, there is a lap joint plus an open mortise through which the stretcher fits and is wedged with a key. Some

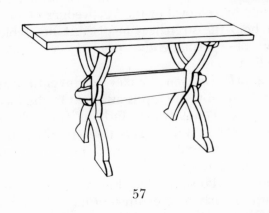

57

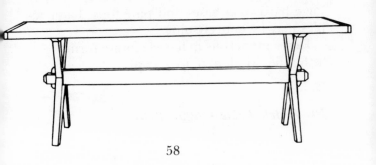

58

tables have two long stretchers that meet each other in a V shape; some have a full-length footrest on each side that is mortised into the legs.

Early sawbuck tables can be dismantled for storage by removal of the key wedges or pegs that hold the stretchers in place. Later tables may be permanently pegged or nailed together.

Fig. 57: Delaware Valley, eighteenth century. Note how the top is attached to the base in typical Pennsylvania fashion with cleats. The scrolling on the legs is also typically Pennsylvania, but similar patterns appear on European tables as well.

Fig. 58: Possibly New England, late eighteenth or early nineteenth century.

Made in all regions. Early tables usually have hardwood bases and pine tops. Later tables may be entirely pine.

Fairly numerous in less elaborate forms such as fig. 58. Mod. exp. to v. exp.

59. Hutch Table (1690–1840)

Is essentially the same as a chair table (figs. 52 and 53) but has a seat wide enough for two or more people. The seat is hinged and opens into a storage hutch. The top is usually rectangular but may also be oval or have rounded corners. The legs and cleats are sometimes scrolled.

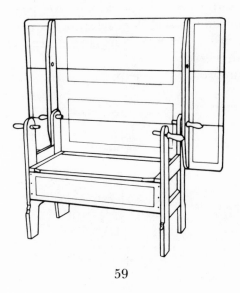

59

Because the cleats extend to the edges of the top, you should expect the underside of the top to be worn on either side of the cleats but hardly worn at all very close to where the cleats are attached.

Hutch tables are sometimes called bench or settle tables.

Fig. 59: Pennsylvania, nineteenth century. Note that the ends of the hutch are paneled, the legs are scrolled, and the underside of the top and front of the hutch are paint decorated—all typical Pennsylvania features.

Made in all regions, usually entirely in pine or other soft woods.

Numerous. Mod. exp. to v. exp.

60

60. Butterfly Table (1700–1735)

Has turned splayed legs connected by stretchers and swing-out leaf supports resembling butterfly wings. The butterfly brackets swing on dowels cut directly into their ends and inserted into holes in the side stretchers and the underside of the central top. The edges of the brackets may have a reverse curve, scrolls, notches (fig. 60), or cutouts. The top is almost always oval with rounded-off edges. The height is 28 inches or less.

As in fig. 60, many butterfly tables have a lipped or flush trapezoidal-shaped drawer in one end of the apron. The drawers are fitted with long wooden knobs instead of brasses.

Butterfly tables are usually considered among the most desirable pieces. They are also among the rarest, and so they are often faked, sometimes from authentic splay-leg tavern tables without drawers (see fig. 50). Wear from people's feet rubbing against the side stretchers of an authentic butterfly table is necessarily uneven because the side stretchers cannot become worn down at their center, where the leaf supports are socketed. Thus a "butterfly table" with evenly worn side stretchers may have begun life as a tavern table.

Fig. 60: Southern New England, 1700–1735.

Made in southern New England, usually entirely in maple, walnut, or cherry, but pine tops or construction entirely in pine are occasionally found.

Rare. V. exp.

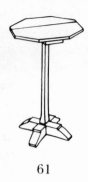

61

61. *X-base Candle Stand (1700–1800)*

Has a round, square, or polygonal top, a turned or chamfered standard, and a base composed of two heavy feet attached to each other in a lap joint at the center.

The standard penetrates the X-base, thus locking together the two cross pieces. The standard may also penetrate the top and be wedged, or it may be stuck into a cleat on the underside of the top. The edge of the top may be flat, rounded, or chamfered.

A variation of this form is the T-base candle stand, which is sometimes called a weaver's stand.

Fig. 61: Probably New England, eighteenth century.

Made in all regions in hard and soft woods.

Not numerous. Mod. exp. to exp.

62

62. Dough Box Table (1700–1840)

Has a single- or multiple-board top with cleats at each end that often slide into dovetail slots. The top rests on a trough that ordinarily has splayed, dovetailed sides. This, in turn, rests on or is attached to a tablelike frame that usually has splayed legs.

The best dough boxes have tops with a good overhang and bases with splayed, turned, stretcher-connected legs, as in fig. 62. Some are far simpler than this one. Of course, the primary function of a dough box was not as a table but as a trough to store rising bread dough. However, the tops were used as work surfaces—for example, for kneading the dough. Also, there are smaller pieces that resemble stands with removable tops that were used in the same way as the larger dough boxes.

Fig. 62: Pennsylvania, 1720–1800. Some of these pieces were paint decorated.

Made primarily in the Pennsylvania region from hard and soft woods.

Numerous, but not in the better forms. Inexp. to exp.

63, 64. Work Table (1700–1840)

Designates any sort of table that was presumably used as a work surface. Of course,

63

such a vague definition encompasses a wide variety of tables. Illustrated are two that are almost always called work tables.

Fig. 63: Hudson Valley, eighteenth century. This is actually a small trestle table. Perhaps the storage cubby under the top was used to hold sewing equipment.

Fig. 64: Probably Northern Shaker, possibly Canterbury, New Hampshire, nineteenth century. Any similar piece may also be called a farm table.

Made in all regions in hard and soft woods.

Common, although pieces like fig. 63 are fairly rare. Inexp. to exp.

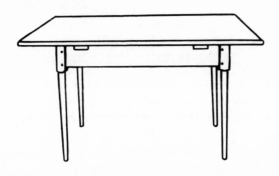

64

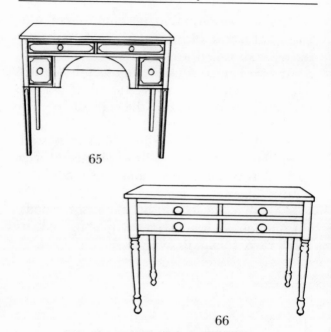

65

66

65, 66. *Serving Table, or Sideboard* *(1720–1840)*

Is a piece that was intended for use in a dining area as a side table. Serving tables earlier than about 1790 usually have no drawers, cupboards, or other elaborations such as serpentine fronts. In country furniture the form really came into its own only after 1790 or so; thus most pieces are in the Hepplewhite or Sheraton styles (figs. 65 and 66, respectively).

Fig. 65: Probably New England, 1800–1830. String inlay was common on similar high-style pieces and may be imitated with paint on country pieces. A similar Southern form with a straight or scrolled apron is called a hunt board.

Fig. 66: Probably New Jersey, 1820–40. Similar pieces are sometimes found in a combination of woods such as cherry tops and legs, poplar sides, and walnut drawer fronts.

Made in all regions in hard and soft woods. Not numerous. Mod. exp. to exp.

67

67. *Half-round Table (1720–1840)*

Has a semicircular top and three or four legs that may be connected by stretchers. The apron is usually rectangular, triangular, or T-shaped.

These pieces are also called wall tables or console tables.

Fig. 67: Probably New England, 1780–1810. Made in all regions in hard and soft woods. Not numerous. Mod. exp. to exp.

68, 69. *Adjustable Candlestand* *(1730–1840)*

Was made in a wide variety of forms, including the screw post (fig. 68), the ratchet (fig. 69), and the sliding with a wooden set screw or wedge. The lower structure varied greatly, too, from the peg leg (figs. 68 and 69) to the X- or T-base (fig. 61), block base, and tripod base (figs. 77–81).

68

On some of these pieces the height of the candle itself may be adjusted with a push- or screw-up device in the candle holder; others have no candle holder at all but a simple block or rod from which a separate hooked candle holder or oil lamp can be hung. Some examples are only about 1½ feet tall and were used on other stands or on tables.

Adjustable candlestands are often faked from bases of old wool winders.

Fig. 68: Possibly New England, eighteenth century. Note how the tray beneath the candle holders is dished out.

Fig. 69: Possibly New England, eighteenth or early nineteenth century.

Made in all regions in hard and soft woods.

Not numerous. Mod. exp. to v. exp.

69

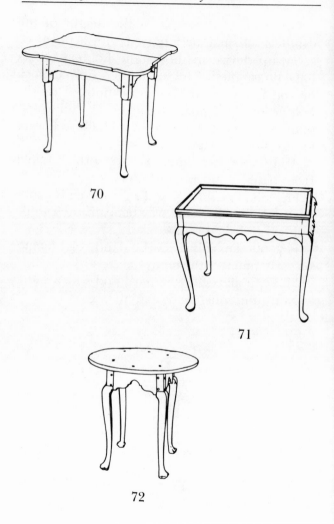

70

71

72

70–72. *Tea Table (1735–1830)*

Usually designates a small, four-legged table in the Queen Anne (sometimes Chippendale) style with a rectangular or round top. The rectangular top is usually 30 to 35 inches long and 20 to 24 inches wide; the round top, about 30 inches in diameter. The top may also be oval, square, or polygonal. The height is usually 26 to 28 inches, i.e., shorter than the full dining height of about 30 inches. The apron may have one or more drawers and may be scrolled. The legs are usually cabriole (fig. 72) or straight cabriole (fig. 70); straight cabriole legs may be splayed.

A common structural feature of authentic tea tables with overhanging tops is a single transverse cleat that runs under the center of the top and through the skirt.

Fig. 70: New England, probably Rhode Island, 1740–1800. This table has what is known as a porringer top, which, along with straight cabriole legs, is associated with Rhode Island. Note how the shaped brackets at the corners of the apron echo the porringer corners of the top.

Fig. 71: New England, possibly Connecticut, 1740–1800. This table has what is known as a tray top, a raised edge formed by applied molding. This type of top is probably the rarest and hence the most sought after.

Fig. 72: Probably New England, possibly Connecticut, 1740–60.

Made in all regions entirely in hard woods or with hardwood bases and pine tops.

Fairly rare. Exp. to v. exp.

73, 74. *Swing-Leg Table (1735–1840)*

Has drop leaves that are supported by hinged, swing-out legs. On smaller four-leg tables, as in figs. 73 and 74, the two diagonally opposite legs swing out. On larger tables there may be six or even eight legs—four stationary

73

legs in the corners and two or four swing legs.

Swing-leg tables are constructed somewhat differently from other drop-leaf tables. The swing legs are attached to the center of the long side of the apron with a wooden finger hinge (fig. 74). Behind this is another board that runs the length of the table—a secondary apron that is dovetailed into the short side of the apron in the corner where the swing leg butts against it when the leaf is down.

Fig. 73: Probably New England, 1740–60.

Fig. 74: Possibly New England, 1760–1800.

Made in all regions with hardwood bases and hardwood or softwood tops.

Numerous, especially in Chippendale and later styles. Inexp. to v. exp.

74

75

75. Card Table (1735–1840)

Is a type of small swing-leg table (see figs. 73 and 74) with a single leaf that can be rested against a wall or folded over the stationary top.

Card tables may have five legs, but country versions usually have four, one or two of which swing out to support the leaf. The top and leaf often have breadboard ends, and the apron often has a drawer, as in fig. 75. Country examples are almost always found in the Chippendale and later styles. It is not unusual to find wear on the bottom of the leaf since, when it is folded over, it becomes the top of the table.

Fig. 75: Possibly New England, 1760–1800. Note how the breadboard ends protrude beyond the edge of the leaf because the leaf has shrunk.

Made in all regions with hardwood bases and hardwood or softwood tops.

Not numerous. Inexp. to v. exp.

76

76. *Pembroke Table (1755–1840)*

Is a small drop-leaf table whose top is essentially square when the leaves are up. The drop leaves are supported by swinging brackets in the apron. The edge of the top may be cut in some variation of a serpentine shape, as in fig. 76—a good indication that the table was made after 1790. Square-leg Chippendale-style Pembroke tables may have flat X-stretchers mortised into the chamfered inner edges of the legs. There may be a drawer in one or both ends of the apron.

Fig. 76: Possibly New England, 1800–1830.

Made in all regions, usually with hardwood bases and hardwood or softwood tops.

Fairly numerous. Inexp. to exp.

77–81. Tripod Table or Stand (1755–1840)

Has three legs attached to a standard and a round, oval, square, rectangular, polygonal, or serpentine top. The top may be stationary, may tip to a vertical position, or may tip and turn. There may be one or more drawers below a stationary top.

A stationary top usually has a round or transverse cleat on its underside. A dowel cut directly on the end of the standard fits into a hole in the cleat. Shaker tables may have threaded dowels and cleats. On some simple tables and stands, the dowel simply runs through the top. A stationary top may also be attached with nails to two lap-joined, X-shaped cleats that are mortised into the top of the standard.

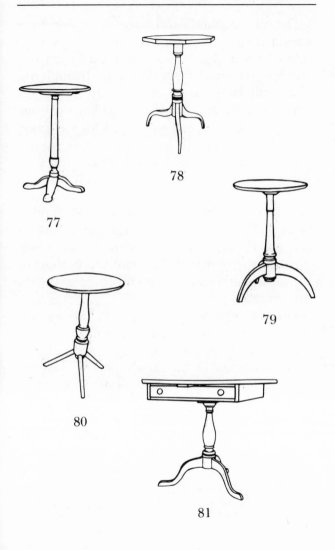

77

78

79

80

81

On tip-top stands and tables, the top of the standard ends in a block of wood. The underside of the top has two transverse cleats that are hinged with a wooden pin through the block, allowing the top to tip vertically. There may also be a brass catch, a wooden turn button, or a sliding dowel to hold the top in a horizontal position.

On tip-and-turn tables and stands, the standard usually ends in a so-called birdcage—a block with four small turned posts stuck into it, which are in turn doweled into another block. The birdcage, which can rotate on the end of the standard, is held by a key wedge through the standard. The tabletop is attached to the upper block of the birdcage as in the tip-top table.

On peg leg stands, like fig. 80, the legs are simply stuck into the standard. Other types of legs usually slide into single open dovetails cut into the bottom of the standard. The dovetails may be covered by a three-spoke iron brace that is nailed or screwed into the underside of the legs. The legs may also be attached with screws, nails, or mortise-and-tenon joints, but those are much weaker forms of construction since the legs tend to spread apart and break out of the standard.

A turned drop at the bottom of the standard

is rare on American tripod tables, but some Shaker tables have turnings or large buttons (figs. 79 and 80). Also, Shaker tripod tables may have tops whose height can be adjusted with a wooden set screw.

Tripod stands are often simply called candle stands. They are frequently faked from bed-post turnings.

There are a remarkable number of design variations in this form of furniture. Illustrated are four representative examples, with comments.

Fig. 77: Possibly New England, 1790–1830. This is an amusing and desirable piece because of its great legs, which look like a melted version of those in fig. 81.

Fig. 78: Possibly New England, 1800–1830. The total design of this stand really works: the spider legs are well curved and taper at the ends, and the standard is attractive, its angular central turning echoing the angularity of the octagonal top.

Fig. 79: Northern Shaker, possibly Mount Lebanon, New York, nineteenth century. This is a dignified but dynamic piece, like a rocket poised for takeoff.

Fig. 80: Possibly northern Shaker, 1790–1830. This stand has a standard that is turned better than those of most peg-leg pieces.

Fig. 81: Northern Shaker, possibly Mount Lebanon, New York, nineteenth century. This Shaker sewing or work table has the triple distinction of being beautiful, elegant, and rare.

Made in all regions, usually with hardwood bases and hardwood or softwood tops, but pieces entirely in soft wood are found.

Fairly common. Inexp. to v. exp.

82–84. Bedside Table or Stand (1790–1840)

Is a small, four-legged piece, usually with a square top. There may be one or two drawers and one or two drop leaves.

Because these stands are usually fairly ordinary in design, I have tried to show three that are above average.

Fig. 82: Probably New England, 1810–30. No, this is not an optical illusion; the righthand legs of this stand do splay more than the lefthand ones, and the top is wider on the right side. Perhaps the stand was made to be used in a particular space that required this unusual design. Whatever the reason for it, the overall effect is pretty extraordinary. The teardrop brass is wrong and should be replaced.

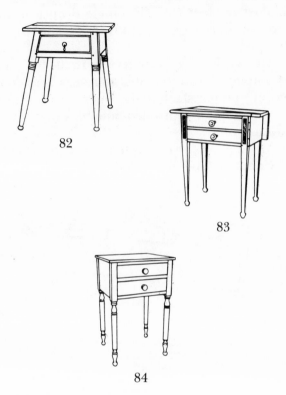

82

83

84

Fig. 83: Probably New England, 1810–30. Most Hepplewhite stands simply have tapered square legs. But look at this one: the legs have angled reeding at the top and ridiculous but terrific flat spade feet that quaintly aspire to high-style elegance. The single drop leaf and two drawers add interest, too. The top is warped.

Fig. 84: Possibly New Jersey, 1820–40. Many examples of country Sheraton legs are either boring or garish, but the ones on this stand have a kind of controlled quietness that is very attractive.

Made in all regions in hard and soft woods. Common. Inexp. to mod. exp.

85

85. Harvest Table (1800–1840)

Usually designates a very long dining table with one or two drop leaves that are supported by swing-out brackets or pull-out slides. There may be a drawer in one or both ends.

Fig. 85: Possibly New England, 1800–1840.

Made in all regions, usually with hardwood bases and pine tops.

Fairly numerous. Mod. exp. to exp.

86

86. Washstand (1800–1840)

In its simplest form has an approximately square top with a shelf drawer about one-half to three-quarters of the way down the legs. Elaborations include more than one drawer, cutouts in the stand top for washing and shaving equipment, a splashboard, and a triangular back allowing the piece to be used in a corner of a room.

Fig. 86: Possibly New England, 1800–1840.

Made in all regions in hard and soft woods.

Common. Inexp. to exp.

87

87. *Dressing Table (1820–40)*

Has a rectangular top, a scrolled backboard or gallery, and one or more drawers. There may also be one or more tiers of drawers on the back of the top.

Fig. 87: Possibly New England, 1820–40.

Made in all regions in hard and soft woods. Common. Inexp. to exp.

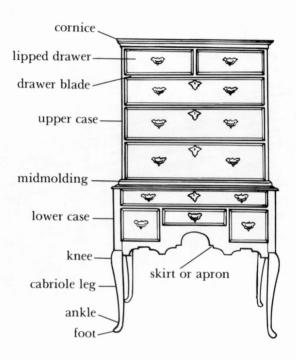

cornice

lipped drawer

drawer blade

upper case

midmolding

lower case

knee

cabriole leg

ankle

foot

skirt or apron

CHESTS AND
CHESTS OF DRAWERS
10

Carcase. This is the total boxlike framework of a case piece minus the drawers, applied molding, etc.

In chests, construction by simply butting and nailing the boards together is found in all periods. In the seventeenth and early eighteenth centuries many chests were constructed by the rail-and-stile (panel) method. The bottoms may be nailed in place. (Paneling of case pieces was revived in the nineteenth century.) In the eighteenth and nineteenth centuries, dovetailing and rabbeting and nailing were used. The lift tops of chests are almost invariably single wide boards, often made of pine even on early paneled oak chests. On the underside of the top at the ends are frequently two transverse cleats; breadboard ends and applied molding are also found. The most common type of hinge used on lift tops is the strap hinge; other types include the cotter-pin, butt, and pintle (wooden dowel) hinges.

Chests of drawers are likely to have dove-tailed tops, sides, and bottoms, but rabbet or mortise-and-tenon joints are also found. The backboards are usually roughly finished, random-width boards connected by lap, tongue-and-groove, or spline joints and nailed in place; backboards are often better finished on the inside of a chest of drawers than on the outside. The tops may be formed in several different ways. On tall pieces, the actual top does not overhang, but molding is applied with pins or brads to form a cornice. On shorter pieces, the tops do overhang and may be nailed, pinned, screwed, or glued in place. On better pieces, there may be a dovetailed subtop beneath the actual top. Drawer separators are often open or blind dovetailed in place, but pinning and nailing are also found.

Highboys and chests-on-chests are made in two separable sections, or an upper and lower case. The upper case usually fits into a mid-molding applied to the top of the lower case, but on some pieces—from Rhode Island, for example—the midmolding may be attached to the bottom of the upper case, which fits over the top of the lower case.

Legs and feet. Many pieces have legs formed by the extension of the corner stiles or corner posts to the floor (figs. 88 and 106, respectively). Cabriole legs are formed essentially the same way, since they are made in one piece with the corner posts, to which the apron and sides are mortised and pinned (fig. 100).

Turned ball feet and their variations (fig. 91), and trumpet-turned legs with ball feet (fig. 97), have dowels cut directly on their ends, which are stuck into holes in the carcase. In fig. 97, the foot and leg are separate pieces, the foot being doweled through the stretcher and into the leg. Some chests, notably those from New York, have ball feet in front and boot-jack feet in back, which are connected front to back by narrow boards on which the chest rests but is not attached in any way.

Bracket feet may be formed by the extension of the sides of the piece with an added, often dovetailed, front board (fig. 92). Or they may be part of a separate frame with mitered corners into which the carcase fits (fig. 104). The mitered feet may have reinforcing blocks behind them or the joint may have a spline running through it.

Perhaps the simplest form of leg and foot is formed by the extension of the plank sides of a piece with the bottoms cut away (fig. 89).

Drawers. Regardless of the primary wood that a drawer front is made of, the sides, back, and bottom of the drawer are always made of an easily worked secondary wood such as pine or poplar. This is in direct contrast to the English practice of using oak as a secondary wood, or perhaps deal, a type of pine that is very light in color, with a wider grain and longer striations than American pine.

In a typical seventeenth-century drawer, the sides are rabbeted and nailed to the front and rabbeted or butt joined to the back. Some of these drawers are nailed from the front and back; others are nailed from the sides, in which case the sides are often dished out with a chisel at the spots where the nails enter (which has the same effect as countersinking the nail). Early rabbeted drawers may have lengthwise grooves cut into their sides, which slide along a runner inside the carcase. Although rabbeted drawers with flush bottoms are by no means limited to the seventeenth century, side runner grooves are usually considered to be a feature of only the earliest drawers.

Eighteenth- and nineteenth-century drawers are likely to have the sides, fronts, and backs dovetailed together, although dovetailing in the front and rabbeting in the back is not unusual. An early eighteenth-century drawer may have only single large dovetails with nails through them. As the century progressed, the number of dovetails increased and they became smaller and finer until in the nineteenth century the necks of the dovetails may be so narrow that they sometimes break. The bottoms of dovetailed drawers are usually made like a panel: the edges of the bottom are chamfered, and the bottom fits into grooves cut into the inner edges of the front and sides. The undersides of the bottoms are usually left roughly finished.

Molding. Cock-beading is a type of applied molding associated with drawers. From head-on, it looks like a narrow, slightly projecting half-round molding. Actually, it is a thin, flat piece of wood whose leading edge is rounded. It is found around some drawer fronts of William and Mary pieces, 1690–1735. Since it is applied molding, it can hide the dovetails that attach the drawer fronts to the sides, although on a drawer its primary purpose is to protect the edges of veneer. About 1735, cock-beaded drawers were abandoned for drawers with lipped front edges, which hid the opening around the drawer. During the Chippendale period, 1755–95, cock-beading was again used, but this time it was attached to the case around the drawer rather than to the drawer itself. Then, from about 1790 on, it was again applied around both veneered and solid drawer fronts. Cock-beading is often imitated on country pieces with a simpler, run-in beading, which, of course, does not project from the surface of the drawer front.

The tops of chests and chests of drawers and the fronts of lipped drawers often have a run-in thumbnail molding. The molding on tops and the rest of the carcase may also be applied, usually with pins or brads.

Veneer. Veneer is not necessarily an indication of inferior workmanship. On the contrary, it is found on some of the best high-style furniture in all periods—hand cut and sometimes over an eighth of an inch thick—although Queen Anne and Chippendale furniture are more likely to be made of solid woods. Veneer is not a common feature of country furniture but is sometimes imitated with paint.

EXAMINATION CHECKLIST

Chests

1. Is the top original? First, check the hinges. If they are original, there will be no extra holes in the top or the back indicating that the hinges have been switched, and there will be no marks or outlines of any other type of hinge. Often, however, the hinges have

been replaced. In that case, the marks left by the original hinges should be consistent on the top and the back. The following are also good items to check.

The fit of the top: The molding or cleats on the top usually fit fairly snugly around the sides. If the fit is very loose, it may indicate a replacement. Similarly, there may be indications that the molding or cleats have been removed to make a top fit on a piece that is too large for it.

The wood: The top, sides, and front are usually made of the same wood.

Planing marks: The inside faces of the boards should all feel about the same.

Color: The underside of the top should have about the same color as the inside faces of the front, sides, and back.

Paint: The top should have the same paint history as the front and sides.

Chests and Chests of Drawers

2. Are the drawers right? Does the color on the sides, back, and bottom match on the inside and outside of the drawers? Is there any evidence of staining, varnishing, or painting to make the drawer parts the same color? There shouldn't be, since drawers were never finished on the inside. Are similar secondary

woods used on all the drawers? Are the top edges of the sides of the drawers shaped in the same way? Is the construction of all the drawers the same, including, for example, the shape of the dovetails or rabbets and the method of attachment of the bottoms to the sides and backs? Are the drawer fronts made from the same wood with similar graining? Is there a glue line around the outer edges of the drawer fronts—an indication that the drawer fronts may be new? Are the marks for the present and/or original brasses consistent on the inside and outside of the drawer fronts, including the distance between the two holes left by brasses that may have been removed? Is there evidence of wear on the drawers—for example, on the bottom edges of the sides? Does the wear correspond to a worn surface inside the carcase that the drawers slide on?

3. Is the color of the wood inside the carcase consistent—for example, where the sides meet the top? Is there any evidence of refinishing to achieve color consistency?

4. Are the legs and feet original? Do they show the proper dotage? Are ball feet slightly out of round? Is there any indication anywhere outside *or* inside the piece that the legs have been spliced? Are there any fresh saw cuts? Also, cabriole legs are sometimes added

to William and Mary pieces that originally had trumpet-turned legs; ball feet are sometimes added to pieces that originally had legs formed from extended corner stiles; bracket-foot bases are sometimes added to highboy tops to make them into tall chests of drawers. . . . The list could go on.

5. Is the molding original? Does it have the irregularities of hand planing? Is it held in place with pins or square-headed brads (the brad holes may be covered with putty, but then the putty holes should be square)?

6. Is there any evidence of new carving, e.g., of fans, to "improve" the piece?

7. Do the backboards match each other in color, method of attachment, joints, finish, feel, etc.? It is especially important to check this on pieces with separate upper and lower cases that may be married. Backboards, of course, should never be varnished, stained, painted, or the like to disguise their appearance.

8. Is the piece right as a whole? Fakers have been known to take an Empire chest of drawers, ca. 1830, remove the heavy projecting front pieces, add bracket feet, and presto!—a Chippendale chest of drawers, ca. 1770. For one thing, the shape of the drawer dovetails in such a piece would be all wrong,

i.e., much narrower than in an authentic Chippendale piece.

(Note: With some two-part country pieces, like chests on chests, the upper and lower cases may have been made at different times but by the same craftsman or group of craftsmen, perhaps because the buyer could not afford both parts at the same time. This probably constitutes a "legal marriage," but it would take expert knowledge to determine.)

88–90. Chest (1670–1840)

Is a box, with or without legs and feet, with a hinged lid. The interior usually has a till, a small, built-in storage compartment with a dowel-hinged lid (see fig. 90). Blanket chest is a common name for almost any chest.

Most chests are simple, with no decoration except for paint and molding. Therefore, any sort of decoration—carving, elaborate or early molding, grain painting, well-scrolled feet, interior drawers, etc.—generally makes the piece more desirable.

Fig. 88: Massachusetts, 1670–1710. This is a rare and probably very expensive paneled and carved oak chest with a pine lid.

Fig. 89: New England, 1670–1710. This is an early so-called six-board chest that is simply

88

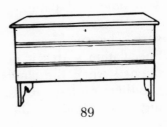

89

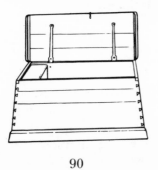

90

nailed together. Two horizontal lines of shadow molding and chip carving are the decoration. The basic form of this chest is common, but early chests like this are not numerous.

Fig. 90: Possibly New England, nineteenth century. This is a dovetailed sea chest with strap hinges on the lid and a till at the left side of the interior. Sea chests often have this trapezoidal shape and rope handles at the ends called beckets. They are frequently decorated, sometimes with paintings of ships or with carving. Interestingly, no one seems to know for sure why sea chests were shaped this way. Speculation is that it permitted the lids to be opened when the chests were standing close together; perhaps it also allowed easier loading in the hold of the ship, with its curved walls.

Made in all regions in hard and soft woods.

Common to rare. V. inexp. to v. exp.

91–93. *Chest over Drawer or Drawers*
(1680–1840)

Has an upper section that is a chest with a lift top plus one or more tiers of drawers below. Sometimes one or more of the drawers are simply false fronts, giving the piece the appearance of a true chest of drawers.

91

92

93

Fig. 91: New England, 1700–1720. The two upper drawers of this piece are really false fronts, as are those of fig. 92. It has single-arch molding around the drawers, usually considered the earliest type of molding on William and Mary pieces.

Fig. 92: New England, 1730–50. Note how the brackets that form the front feet are dovetailed into the extension of the sides.

Fig. 93: Pennsylvania, 1780–1800. Chests similar to this one were made in various rural counties of Pennsylvania from about 1760 to 1830 (this one may be from Berks County). They are called dower chests, especially when a woman's name appears on them. Chests made in soft wood were decorated with paint in various designs, including unicorns, birds, fish, tulips, horsemen, and hex signs. Chests made in hard woods such as walnut were not painted but sometimes have wooden or wax inlays.

Made in all regions in hard and soft woods.

Numerous. Mod. exp. to v. exp.

94, 95. *Early Chest of Drawers (1690–1710)*

Is paneled, usually with four tiers of drawers with wooden knobs or brasses. Some

94

95

sort of applied decoration is standard, such as bosses, split spindles (fig. 94), or geometric molding (fig. 95).

The upper and lower sections of these pieces are actually two separate boxes, the split between them hidden with a molding strip. They were painted, often red and black, to emphasize the applied decoration.

Fig. 94: New England, probably Massachusetts, 1690–1710. The top tier of drawers on this piece is split into two separate drawers.

Fig. 95: New England, probably Massachusetts, 1690–1710.

Made primarily in New England, usually in hard woods.

Rare. V. exp.

96. *William and Mary Chest of Drawers* *(1700–1735)*

Has four to six tiers of drawers, with the top tier usually split into two drawers. Ordinarily the drawers are surrounded with double-arch molding, as in fig. 97; lipped drawers, as in fig. 96, are less common and a late feature. There is usually heavy applied molding on the top and base.

96

These pieces were also made in the chest on frame form (see fig. 102).

Fig. 96: New England, 1720–35.

Made in all regions in hard and soft woods. Not numerous. Exp. to v. exp.

97

98

99

97–99. *Highboy (1700–1810)*

Is basically a chest of drawers supported on another chest of drawers with long legs.

William and Mary highboys (fig. 97) have flat tops with cornice molding ranging from quite simple to elaborate and heavy. Sometimes there is a "secret" drawer just above the last tier of drawers that is masked by a torus molding, as in fig. 97. The midmolding is invariably heavy. The base is supported by trumpet-turned legs and ball feet. The typical piece has four front legs and two rear legs; rarely are there only two or three front legs. When the piece has flat box stretchers, they usually conform in shape to the arches and scrolls of the lower edge of the bottom section, which is often covered with an applied cockbead molding (fig. 97). Typically, the upper case has four tiers of graduated drawers, the top tier being split; the lower case may have from one to two tiers of one to four drawers each, one tier of three drawers being the most common, as in fig. 97. A lower case with no drawers is very rare. William and Mary highboys were often veneered. Note that these pieces are quite short, ranging from 4 feet to 5 feet 5 inches tall.

Country Queen Anne highboys usually have flat tops, but scrolled and broken arch bonnet tops are also found. The upper case may have from four to as many as six graduated drawers. The top tier or top two tiers may not be full width. The top drawers may also be separated by a narrower drawer with fan, shell, sunburst, or other carved decoration. The lower case usually has a drawer arrangement as in fig. 98, although there are other arrangements; sometimes there is a carved decoration. The drawers are often, but not always, lipped, with thumbnail molding. The lower case is supported by cabriole legs, ending in some form of pad foot. The apron is scrolled and may have two turned drops, supposedly a holdover of the "missing" two middle legs from the William and Mary style. Some Rhode Island pieces may have a third drop in the center of the apron. These pieces can be more than 7 feet tall.

Chippendale highboys usually have lipped drawers (fig. 99). There are almost always five tiers in the upper case and up to three tiers in the lower case, giving a more massive appearance than the Queen Anne style. The feet, too, are usually more massive, ranging from claw-and-ball to trifid (fig. 99) to a heavy pad. These pieces are stylistic variations of the Queen Anne form.

Fig. 97: New England, 1700–1735.

Fig. 98: New England, probably Massachusetts, 1740–60.

Fig. 99: Pennsylvania, 1755–1810.

Made in all regions, usually in hard woods.

Fairly numerous. V. exp.

100

100. Lowboy (1700–1810)

Is stylistically the same as a highboy of the period in which it was made and superficially resembles the lower case of a highboy (figs. 97–99). But whereas a highboy base may be over 46 inches wide, a lowboy is typically less than 36 inches wide.

Lowboys, of course, were made as companion pieces to highboys.

Fig. 100: New England, probably Massachusetts, 1740–60.

Made in all regions, usually of hard woods.

Fairly numerous. Exp. to v. exp.

101

102

101, 102. *Queen Anne Chest of Drawers (1735–60)*

Has four or five tiers of drawers on a low base.

Fig. 101: New England, 1735–50. This is a rare form of American furniture. If you compare it with the upper case of fig. 98, you will see just how easy it is to fake: all that is needed is a highboy top to which bracket feet have been added. Thus the base of such a piece claimed to be all original should be examined with extreme care.

Fig. 102: New England, 1740–60. This simple but interesting country piece could also be called a chest on frame since the top section is separate from the lower section. The drawers never had brasses or knobs.

Made in New England, usually in hard woods.

Rare. Exp. to v. exp.

103. Chest on Chest (1755–1840)

Is basically a chest of drawers supported by another chest of drawers, i.e., a highboy with more or deeper drawers in the lower case. The upper case has four or five tiers of graduated drawers and the lower case from two to four tiers. The tops of country chests on chests are usually flat.

This is a form that began in the Chippendale period and remained popular into the early nineteenth century.

103

Fig. 103: Probably New England, 1755–1810. Compare this with the linen press, fig. 130.

Made in all regions, usually in hard woods. Fairly numerous. Exp. to v. exp.

104

105

106

107

104–107. Chest of Drawers (1755–1840)

Is simply several tiers of drawers on legs.

The chest of drawers really came into its own in America in the Chippendale period. Country examples usually have straight fronts, but bowed, serpentine, and oxbow fronts are also found. When the top drawer is deeper than the other drawers, contrary to the way drawers are usually graduated, it is often called a bonnet drawer, the presumption being, of course, that bonnets were stored there.

Fig. 104: New England, 1760–1810. Chests with six or more tiers of drawers are sometimes called tall chests.

Fig. 105: Probably New England,

1800–1830. Note the French feet and valanced apron on this well-proportioned piece.

Figs. 106 and 107: New England, probably Maine, 1810–30 and 1810–50, respectively. These are so-called State o' Maine chests, which were made in the Sheraton (fig. 107) and, less frequently, in the Hepplewhite (fig. 106) styles. The carcases are basically just glued and nailed together, which, of course, does not lessen their charm for those who like this sort of object.

Made in all regions in hard and soft woods.

Common. Inexp. to v. exp.

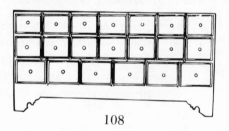

108

108. Apothecary Chest (1755–1840)

Is a chest of many small drawers with or without legs. It resembles a large spice chest.

Fig. 108: Probably New England, 1760–1820.

Made in all regions, frequently in pine.

Fairly numerous. Mod. exp. to exp.

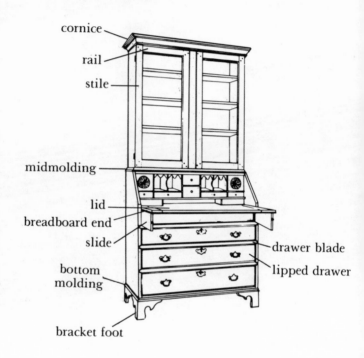

cornice

rail

stile

midmolding

lid

breadboard end

slide

bottom
molding

bracket foot

drawer blade

lipped drawer

DESKS
11

CONSTRUCTION

Lid. A simple desk lid may be nothing more than a single wide board. In better construction, the lid consists of one or more boards with breadboard ends. Some nineteenth-century lids are made in panel construction. The edge of the lid has a run-in thumbnail molding on its edges and is cut out on its inner edges in a lip that overlaps the carcase when the lid is closed. Lids that fold forward are usually hinged at the bottom with butt hinges. Lids that open upward usually have butt hinges, but other types, such as butterfly and cotter-pin, are also found, especially on early pieces.

Drawers. Small interior drawers are often dovetailed together. The bottoms may be flush and nailed or attached with tiny wooden pins. Rabbeted and nailed drawers are also found. A time-honored touchstone for the excellence of construction of interior drawers is removing them and replacing them upside down: if they operate just as well that way as right side up, they are considered well made.

Large drawers are constructed in the same way as those in chests of drawers. See Chapter 10, p. 237.

Secret compartments. Any movable or removable part of the interior may conceal a secret compartment or drawer. These include a sliding or lift-out panel in the top of the interior writing surface that gives access to a recess below (this may be obvious even with the lid closed since there will be a wide space between the top drawer of the exterior and the lower edge of the slant lid, as in fig. 111); tall, narrow document drawers that may be disguised with pilasters, split spindles, and the like; drawers or compartments behind removable lockers; compartments behind drawers; compartments behind sliding pigeonhole arches; and even compartments reached from the back of the desk.

Slides. Slides that support the writing surface lid must be pulled out manually. They are usually rectangular, but may be square on early or Rhode Island pieces (fig. 111). They have some sort of wooden or brass knob at the end; a wooden knob may be cut directly on the end of the slide. Sometimes the ends of the slides are lipped (fig. 112).

Carcase. Desk carcases are constructed in the

same way as those of chests of drawers. See Chapter 10, p. 235.

Feet and legs. Same as on chests of drawers.

Secretary tops. These are usually, but not always, separable from the bottom section. Removable tops usually fit into applied molding around the top of the lower section. They are constructed either like the carcases of chests of drawers or like cupboards. For the latter, see Chapter 12, p. 283.

Frame. The frame of a desk on frame, schoolmaster's desk, etc., is constructed like a table in the same style. See Chapter 9, p. 193.

Molding. Same as on chests of drawers.

Veneer. Same as on chests of drawers.

EXAMINATION CHECKLIST

1. In schoolmaster's desks (fig. 120), is there any evidence that the desk box section was once a separate counter-top desk to which legs have been added? For example, the apron should be mortised into the legs. Is it, or do the legs simply penetrate the bottom of the desk and attach to the sides with screws or nails?

2. In desks on frames (fig. 110), were the frame and the desk box made for each other, or are they married? Check items such as con-

struction methods, wear, woods, general style, paint history, etc.

3. Is the lid original? Are the outer edges of the lid molded, not simply chamfered? Are the hinge marks on the lid and the carcase consistent? Is the lid made of the same wood as the carcase (it usually is)? If there is a lock on the lid, does it correspond to the lock plate on the carcase?

4. Does the lid have any inlay that is not original? This may be difficult to detect unless the inlay work is much sloppier than the general construction of the piece.

5. Are the slides original, or have one or both of them been replaced? Are they finished in the same way and do their edges and ends show similar wear?

6. Is it possible that the slides are not original at all, but that a desk with a lid that opens upward has been converted to a drop lid desk? Check to see if there is evidence of hinges at the *top* of the lid and carcase. Check the opening for the slides for new saw cuts.

7. If there are interior drawers, do they all operate as well upside down as right side up? If not, perhaps the drawers that do not work well upside down are new.

For more points to check on drawers, see the examination checklist for chests of drawers, p. 241, item 2.

8. On secretaries with removable tops, is there any evidence that the top is too big or too small for the lower section, i.e, that the piece is a marriage? Does the top overhang in the back (this is almost never true of authentic pieces)? Is the top too narrow or shallow for the lower section? Can you see any of the dovetails in the top of the lower section? If so, why? (Note: The overall dimensions of removable secretary tops are usually half as deep as the lower section and 1½ to 3 inches narrower.)

For more points to check on secretary tops, see the examination checklist for cupboards, p. 286, items 2 and 3.

9. Finally, remember that it is possible to build an entirely new desk around a good set of early interior drawers. The construction methods and quality of the interior should match those of the desk as a whole.

109

109. Writing or Bible Box (1660–1840)

Is like a small chest that may or may not have feet. The top may be parallel to the base or may slant, in which case the piece may be called a desk box or traveling desk. True writing boxes are relatively small, about 18 to 26 inches wide. Larger boxes, 30 or so inches wide and resembling the upper part of fig. 120, are really counter-top desks.

The earliest writing boxes are often decorated with paint, representational or geometric carving, or bosses and split spindles. After about 1735, writing boxes are usually plain. Nineteenth-century writing boxes are sometimes hinged in the middle and open flat to form a writing surface below which are pigeonholes, drawers, etc.

The term "Bible box" is often applied to writing boxes with no locks, the assumption being that no one would steal a Bible!

Fig. 109: Probably Massachusetts or Connecticut, 1680–1710. This rare piece has the famous shallow Hadley-style carving—featuring leaves, scrolls, and tulips—that is also found on the so-called Hadley chests. Note the cotter-pin hinges.

Early writing boxes are associated with Massachusetts and Connecticut and are usually made in oak or pine with pine tops. Later pieces were made in all regions in hard and soft woods.

Early pieces are rare, later ones fairly numerous. Inexp. to v. exp.

110

110. Desk on Frame (1690–1840)

Is essentially a desk box that sits on a table-like frame usually having one tier of one to three drawers. In addition, the desk-box section may have a drawer. Traditionally the frame section has a molding around its upper edge into which the desk-box section fits (see fig. 115); in late eighteenth- and nineteenth-century pieces, the desk box may overhang the frame, as in fig. 110. The interior may be fitted with drawers, pigeonholes, lockers, etc.

In the early desks on frames, the lid was hinged at the back. Around 1700, lids began to be hinged at the front and swung forward to form a writing surface that rested on pull-out slides. After about 1735, the form became unpopular but was revived toward the end of the eighteenth century.

Some of these pieces are more than 40 inches tall and must be used with a tall stool or standing up. This form is sometimes called a countinghouse desk.

Fig. 110: Probably New England, 1780–1820. Although this piece may have been made in the nineteenth century, its lid is hinged in the back, reverting to a style of a hundred years earlier (as does the schoolmaster's desk, fig. 120).

Made in all regions in hard and soft woods.

Rare to fairly numerous. Mod. exp. to v. exp.

111–13. *Slant-Lid Desk* (*1700–1840*)

Has a lid that slants at about a 45-degree angle. The lid folds forward to form a writing surface that rests on pullout slides (on simple pieces, the lid may rest on the edge of the pulled-out top drawer). Below the lid are three or four tiers of drawers, usually graduated. The fronts of country pieces are ordinarily flat but may be serpentine or oxbow (fig. 113). The interiors may be fitted with drawers, pigeonholes, document holders, lockers, etc.

Decorative treatments include shell carving,

scrolled skirts, turned drops, inlaid lids, grain painting, and the like.

Fig. 111: New England, 1715–35. Note the space between the upper drawer and the lid to allow for the secret compartment below the writing surface.

Fig. 112: New England, possibly New

111

112

113

Hampshire, 1770–1800. At first glance, this piece may seem to have Queen Anne cabriole legs. However, these squat, "bandy" legs are a Chippendale type. Similar legs are found on pieces made by the Dunlap craftsmen of New Hampshire.

Fig.   113:   Probably   New   England, 1790–1820. Although serpentine and reverse-serpentine (oxbow) fronts were also used on Chippendale case pieces, on country furniture such curved fronts are almost always found on Hepplewhite pieces, as here.

114

Made in all regions, usually in hard woods such as maple, cherry, walnut, and birch.

Fairly numerous. Exp. to v. exp.

114–16. *Secretary Desk (1700–1840)*

Is usually made in two parts: a bottom section that looks like a slant-lid desk and an upper bookcase or cupboard section. There are other variations, however, such as fig. 115, which is a desk on frame, and fig. 116, whose lid does not slant sharply enough to qualify as

115   116

a slant-lid desk. In some simple country pieces, the bookcase section is made in one piece with the slant-lid section.

The bookcase may be glazed, paneled, or simply have plank doors. High-style pieces may have scrolled or bonnet tops, but country pieces usually have flat tops.

Fig. 114: New England, probably Connecticut or Massachusetts, 1760–1800. The wooden paneled doors of the bookcase have been replaced with glass.

Fig. 115: Possibly New England, 1800–1830. With the simplicity and proportions reminiscent of some Shaker pieces, this secretary shows much of the excitement and ingenuity that country furniture can have. Consider the parts from top to bottom: a bookcase, a desk box as in a desk on frame, a drawer, a pullout writing slide, and a shelf over a storage hutch!

Fig. 116: Probably northern New England, 1820–40. Compare this piece with the State o' Maine chests, figs. 106 and 107.

Made in all regions, usually in hard woods such as maple, walnut, cherry, and birch.

Fairly numerous. Mod. exp. to v. exp.

117. *Tambour Desk (1790–1840)*

Has a top section with sliding doors composed of thin strips of wood glued to a fabric backing, usually canvas. Frequently there is a central locker that is not covered by the sliding doors. The interior may be fitted with pigeonholes, drawers, and document holders. Below the tambour section is a hinged writing flap that folds forward and rests on pullout slides. The lower section has one to four drawers (usually graduated if there is more than one drawer).

On some pieces there is a tier of shallow drawers above the tambour section; other pieces may be made like a secretary, with a bookcase above the tambour section. In some country pieces, the tambour doors are simply ordinary hinged cupboard doors that may be reeded to look like tambour shutters. This type of piece is sometimes called a blind door secretary.

117

Fig. 117: Probably New England, 1790–1830.

Made primarily in New England, usually in hard woods. Some pieces may be veneered.

Not numerous with true tambour shutters. V. exp.

118, 119. Fall-Front Desk (1790–1840)

Has a top section with a hinged vertical lid that falls forward to form a writing surface, but these desks do not have pullout slides. In addition, the top of the top section may be hinged like a chest lid and give access to a storage area. The interior may be fitted with pigeonholes, drawers, shelves, lockers, document holders, etc. Below the top section are

118

one to four tiers of drawers (usually graduated if there is more than one drawer).

On rare occasions in country furniture this type of desk is made so that the writing surface can be pulled out about half its length, and the fall front is supported by two quarter-round brass brackets at each end. This sort of desk, which looks like a chest of drawers when closed, and pieces like fig. 118 are sometimes called butler's desks or chests.

Fig. 118: Possibly New England, 1800–1840. This desk, of course, would have to be used while standing up.

Fig. 119: Possibly New England, 1810–40. This is essentially a table with a box on it.

Made in all regions, usually in hard woods.

Numerous. Mod. exp. to exp.

119

120

120. *Schoolmaster's Desk* (1800–1840)

Is essentially a desk box with legs. The lid is hinged at the rear and swings upward. Below the desk box there may be a drawer. The top may have a gallery, and the front edge of the slanting lid may have a raised edge to prevent books or papers from sliding off (fig. 120). The interior may be fitted with drawers and pigeonholes but is frequently plain.

Tall versions of these desks that must be used with a tall stool or while standing up are usually called countinghouse or store desks.

Fig. 120: Possibly New England, 1800–1830.

Made in all regions, often with a pine desk box and hardwood legs.

Common. Inexp. to mod. exp.

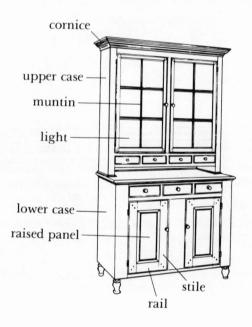

cornice

upper case

muntin

light

lower case

raised panel

stile

rail

CUPBOARDS
12

CONSTRUCTION

Carcase. This is the total boxlike framework of a case piece minus the doors, drawers, applied molding, etc.

Some cupboards are dovetailed together. However, the only parts of a typical cupboard carcase that are likely to be dovetailed are the top of a piece with applied cornice molding, the top of the lower case of a two-part corner cupboard, and the sink part of a lift-top dry sink. The rest of the carcase is held together with nailed butt joints (especially built-in, or architectural, corner cupboards and simple pieces), nailed or pinned rabbet joints, or pinned stiles and rails (especially kases and schranks). Unless they are paneled, the sides of cupboards are almost always made of single boards. The backboards are nailed in place, usually run vertically, and are connected by butt, lap, tongue-and-groove, or spline joints; they are more roughly finished on the outside of the cupboard than on the inside. The separable upper and lower cases of two-part cupboards may fit together in two basic ways: the upper case may rest on the lower case and fit into an applied molding, or the ends of the sides of the upper case may fit into mortises in the top of the lower case.

Doors. Simple doors may be single boards, sometimes with breadboard ends; or they may be multiple boards connected by some sort of joint and held together with transverse cleats nailed or screwed in place. In paneled doors the panels are usually raised, or chamfered, on the outside or inside (diamond-shaped raised panels may indicate a Canadian origin). When the stiles and rails are pinned, there may be up to four pins at each joint, staggered to avoid splitting the wood. Stiles and rails may also be held fast by gluing or by a wedge hammered through an open mortise in the stile into the tenon of the rail. Glazed doors almost always have multiple panes of glass. The panes are held in place by vertical and horizontal strips of wood called muntins, which are mortised into the rails and stiles. Note that the horizontal muntins *always* align with the shelves behind them, hiding the shelves' front edges from view.

Cupboard doors are hung with a wide variety of hinges including butt, rattail, H, HL, butterfly, and cotter-pin hinges. Another type of wrought iron hinge has a pintle section that ends in a sharp point, which is hammered into the door frame.

Shelves. Shelves usually slide into grooves cut into the sides of the cupboard, where they are pinned or nailed in place. In simple construction, shelves may only be nailed. They may also rest on blocks of wood. Elaborations include plate rails or grooves, spoon slots, scrolled front edges (corner cupboards), and molded front edges.

Drawers, legs, feet, and molding. Cupboard drawers are somewhat more likely to be rabbeted and nailed together than the drawers of other forms of furniture. Apart from this, they and the legs, feet, and molding are constructed in the same way as those of chests and chests of drawers. See Chapter 10, pp. 236–40.

EXAMINATION CHECKLIST

1. In cupboards with unpaneled sides, are the sides made from single boards? They usually are, except in corner cupboards. Multiple boards may indicate some reworking or a fake.

2. On two-part cupboards, are the construction method and decorative treatment the same or consistent on both parts? Are the backboards the same color and finished the same way? Is there any evidence that the two parts have been refinished or repainted to match each other in color?

3. On cupboards with doors, are the doors original? Have any of the doors been stained or repainted to match the other doors in color? Do the backs of the doors feel as though they have been finished in a similar way to the inside of the sides? Is the decorative treatment on the top and bottom doors the same (beading, molding, size of pins, etc.)? Are the hinge marks and/or chiseled out holes for the hinges consistent on the door and frame? Is there a slot under the center front edge of any of the shelves into which a turn button on the inside

of any of the doors would fit to hold the doors shut, but no turn button or indication of one on any of the doors? Similarly, is there a turn button or indication of one on the inside of any of the doors, but no slot under any shelf? On paneled doors, do any of the panels seem to have been cut down, e.g., are all four edges of the chamfering the same on all the doors? In glazed doors, do the muntins line up with the edges of the shelves? If they do not, it could mean that the doors are not original or that wood panels have been replaced with glass panes. In addition, do all the panes of glass have the same optical qualities? (Of course, it is unusual to find an antique cupboard whose glazed doors have all their original panes of old glass.)

4. On open cupboards, is there any evidence that the piece originally had doors? For example, have small blocks of wood been used to fill in the hinge mortises on the door frames?

5. Is there any evidence of new saw cuts or new nails, especially on any areas that are scrolled or curved?

6. See also the appropriate items in the examination checklist for chests and chests of drawers, Chapter 10, pp. 241–44.

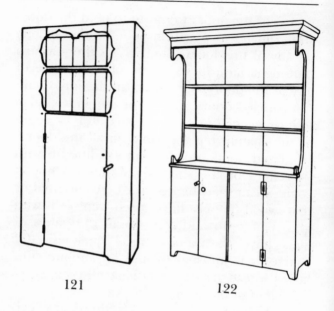

121   122

121–123. *Open Cupboard (1700–1840)*

Has a doorless top section with two or more
shelves above a lower section that is a closed
cupboard, also usually containing shelves. The
top and bottom may be one piece or made in
two separable parts.

Open cupboards are sometimes called
dressers or pewter cupboards. Pieces like fig.
123 are often called Welsh dressers.

Fig. 121: New England, late eighteenth or

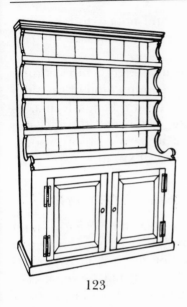

123

early nineteenth century. The reverse curves in the upper section of this piece are a typical New England motif. This is a type of cupboard that is often faked.

Fig. 122: New England, late eighteenth or early nineteenth century. This is a standard design of many New England open cupboards but nevertheless an elegantly simple one. The C-curves on the sides and the canopy are reminiscent of some settles. Note the two-board door, whose only decoration is a narrow beading down the center, and notice, too, how the simple, cutout feet echo the lines of the cornice.

Fig. 123: Pennsylvania, eighteenth century. The knoblike scrolled continuation of the sides is a feature associated with Pennsylvania, as are spoon slots in one or more of the shelves.

Made in all regions in hard and soft woods.

Not numerous to rare. Exp. to v. exp.

124, 125. Corner Cupboard (1730–1840)

Has a back made so that the piece can stand in a corner of a room. The back may come to a point, may have one or more boards parallel to the front of the piece, or may be semicircular (barrel back). The top and bottom sections may be made in two parts, as in fig. 125. The bottom section is usually a closed cupboard. There may be one or more drawers, almost always in the bottom section.

Many corner cupboards were architectural; that is, they were built into the corner of a room as part of the interior architecture. This type of cupboard has no feet, its bottom molding resting directly on the floor. Because of their obvious efficiency in space utilization, corner cupboards were a very popular form of furniture. They still are.

124   125

Fig. 124: New England, 1740–1800. Shelves scrolled like these are sometimes called butterfly shelves.

Fig. 125: Probably Pennsylvania, 1820–50. The unequal width drawers and large knobs are typical of Pennsylvania, as are ball feet on so late a piece (but note that the shape of the feet is very different from that of, e.g., fig. 111).

Made in all regions in hard and soft woods.

Numerous. Exp. to v. exp.

126

126, 127. *Kas or Schrank (1700–1840)*

Has a large, wardrobelike upper section with or without shelves over one to three drawers.

Although small kases are known, many of them are elephantine. For example, it is not unusual for a Pennsylvania piece to be 7 to 8 feet tall, 7½ feet wide, and 25 to 30 inches deep. No wonder many kases are held together with removable pins and wedges so

127

that the piece can be completely taken apart for transportation (or to fit through doorways!).

Purists call kases from Pennsylvania "schranks," the German word for wardrobe or cupboard.

Fig. 126: New York, 1755–1810.

Fig. 127: Pennsylvania, 1755–1810.

Made primarily in Pennsylvania, New Jersey, and New York of walnut, red gum, poplar, or pine.

Not numerous. Mod. exp. to v. exp.

128

128, 129. *Closed Cupboard (1780–1840)*

Has doors on both the upper and lower section. The upper and lower sections may be made in two parts, as in figs. 128 and 129. Either or both of the sections may have drawers.

Cupboards like fig. 128 are sometimes called Dutch cupboards; those like fig. 129 are sometimes called step-back cupboards.

Fig. 128: Probably Pennsylvania, 1810–40. This drawer arrangement—four or five small

129

drawers over three large ones—is found on many Pennsylvania pieces. Similar feet are found on Pennsylvania blanket chests. The space below the upper section is often called a pie shelf.

Fig. 129: Possibly Ohio, 1800–1830. The original rattail hinges on this piece might indicate a Pennsylvania origin, but paneling like this was also done in Ohio.

Made in all regions in hard and soft woods.

Numerous. Mod. exp. to v. exp.

130

130. Linen Press (1780–1840)

Has a cupboard upper section and a lower section that is a chest with three to five tiers of graduated drawers. The interior of the cupboard always has shelves and often drawers or slide-out trays.

Linen presses seem to combine the basic ideas of the kas (fig. 126) with the chest on chest (fig. 103). Small paneled cupboards with shelves are also sometimes called linen presses.

Fig. 130: Probably New Jersey, 1780–1800. This piece looks very much like similar pieces attributed to Matthew Egerton of New Jersey.

Made primarily in New Jersey, Pennsylvania, New York, and Connecticut in hard and soft woods.

Not numerous. Mod. exp. to v. exp.

131

131. *"Jelly" Cupboard (1780–1840)*

Generally is a one-piece cupboard with one or two doors and one or two drawers above them. The top often has a low gallery. Most examples are nineteenth century and simple in design.

Although these cupboards must have been used to store things other than jams and jellies, the term "jelly cupboard" is always understood to refer to this type of piece.

Fig. 131: Pennsylvania, 1800–1830. This is really an extraordinary jelly cupboard, with far more elaborate features than most: a cornice with matchstick molding below it, cockbeaded drawers, three-panel door, stop chamfered corners, and a fancy valanced skirt. Such a piece might bring five to ten times the price of an ordinary jelly cupboard.

Made primarily in the Pennsylvania region of pine or poplar.

Common. Mod. exp.

132. Tall Closed Cupboard (1780–1840)

Is up to 6½ feet tall, fairly narrow, and 1 to 2 feet deep. The shelves may be adjustable. Most examples are nineteenth century and simple in design.

Fig. 132: Probably New England, nineteenth century. For some reason New England pieces often seem to be narrower than those from points south. Note the breadboard ends on both edges of the single-board door.

Made in all regions, usually in soft woods.

Common. Inexp. to mod. exp.

133. Shaker Cupboard (1800–1840)

Is usually large with clean, functional lines. Below the upper, closed cupboard section are

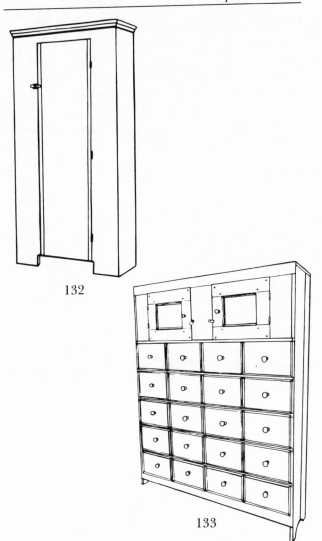

132

133

multiple tiers of drawers. A typical Shaker cupboard has plank sides and doors with flat panels; the rails usually have two staggered pegs at each joint, but a center rail between two panels may have four staggered pegs. The drawers are often lipped and have wooden knobs. The top may have a cornice, but pieces that were built in do not.

Another typical feature of Shaker work is the beading or quarter-round molding around the door panels, which is run into the rails and stiles rather than being applied.

Fig. 133: Northern Shaker, nineteenth century. Shaker cupboards were made in many variations, but this piece conveys the general feeling of most of them.

Made in Shaker communities, usually of knot-free, naturally finished pine. Some pieces are lightly stained red or yellow.

Not numerous. Exp. to v. exp.

134. Bucket, or Water, Bench (1800–1840)

Is usually a closed cupboard below a single raised shelf with a gallery around it. Very simple pieces with an open lower cupboard and no backboards are not unusual, however.

Some Pennsylvania bucket benches may be

up to 5 feet tall and fairly elaborate with scrolled sides and feet and a tier of small drawers below the top shelf. Most, perhaps all, examples are nineteenth century.

Even in their simple forms, these pieces often command prices seemingly far out of proportion to their importance, rarity, or excellence of design.

Fig. 134: Probably Pennsylvania region, nineteenth century. Presumably, kitchen utensils were stored on the top shelf, buckets of water on the shelf above the cupboard, and empty buckets in the cupboard.

Made primarily in the Pennsylvania region in soft woods.

Numerous. Mod. exp. to exp.

134

135

135, 136. Dry Sink (1800–1840)

Is a low closed cupboard with a shallow well above it. The well, or sink, may be formed by extensions of the back and sides and a separate front board (fig. 135), or it may be a separate framework (fig. 136). To make it watertight, the well was usually lined with zinc—not with copper, as in so many reproductions— and dry sinks with their original linings are of course more valuable than those without them. Most examples are nineteenth century and simple in design.

There are many variations, including high backs with cupboards, tall galleries with

136

drawers, front drawers, and lift tops. Nineteenth-century factory-made versions should not be confused with handmade pieces. Note, too, that dry sinks are probably the most often faked, altered, and reproduced form of antique country furniture.

Fig. 135: Probably Pennsylvania region, nineteenth century. This is a typical dry sink—useful but not very interesting.

Fig. 136: New England, nineteenth century. This is a much more interesting piece with its little drawer and separate well, whose sides swoop up to a top shelf.

Made in all regions in soft woods.

Common. Mod. exp. to exp.

137

137. *Lift-top Commode (1800–1840)*

Is a small closed cupboard with a chestlike section above it that usually has a single drawer. There is almost always a midmolding between the cupboard and chest sections that echoes the thumbnail molding on the lift top. These pieces were used to store pitchers, bowls, shaving implements, etc.

Lift-top commodes are probably a good example of a type of case piece that became so popular in handmade versions that furniture factories imitated them. Made at the beginning of the Victorian period—ca. 1840—the factory pieces are always more "curvy" than the handmade pieces; for example, factory pieces often have lift tops with rounded, rather than square, corners, and the aprons have more scrolls.

Fig. 137: Possibly Pennsylvania region, 1810–30.

Made in all regions, usually from soft woods.

Fairly numerous. Inexp. to mod. exp.

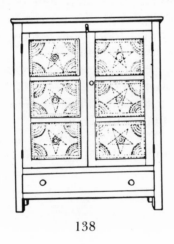

138

138. Pie Safe (1820–40)

Is a closed cupboard whose door panels are formed from hand-pierced pieces of tin or sometimes wire screening. In addition, the sides may have tin panels and there may be one or more drawers in the top or bottom of the piece. Some pie safes are made in the form of step-back cupboards (fig. 129), and others may be very elaborate with a combination of glazed and tin-paneled doors.

Generally these pieces are not very interesting except for the tin panels, which were pierced in a variety of patterns including birds, flowers, vases, and geometric designs. Among other things, the tin panels were supposed to protect food from insects. They may be pierced inward or outward.

Pie safes were made in quantity by furniture factories, often in oak.

Fig. 138: Possibly Pennsylvania, Ohio, or Kentucky, nineteenth century.

Made in all regions, usually in soft woods.

Fairly common. Inexp. to mod. exp.

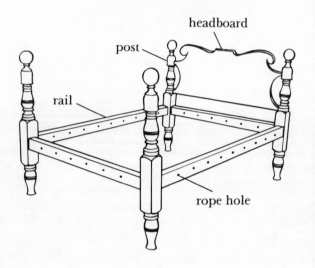

BEDS
13

CONSTRUCTION

Daybeds. Daybeds are constructed basically like chairs in the same style. See the construction notes on chairs, Chapter 6, pp. 123–24.

Beds. Most country beds consist of eight to ten separate parts: four posts, two long rails, two short rails, and possibly a headboard and a footboard. Each rail fits into a mortise in the square section of each post. The end of each rail and the mortises in the posts are often marked with chiseled Roman numerals—I through VIII—to indicate which rail fits into which post. The entire bed is held together by a network of ropes that also serves as the mattress "springs," although some beds have bolts that screw through the posts into the rails. The rope is threaded through holes drilled in the rails or is wound around knobs set into the tops of the rails. Headboards and footboards also fit into mortises in the posts;

they are often made of pine or poplar regardless of the wood used in the rest of the bed.

EXAMINATION CHECKLIST

1. Are the posts hand turned, or, in the case of pencil-post beds, hand carved? Do they show the imperfections associated with handwork? Are they slightly out of round? Do the feet show the proper dotage?

2. Are the posts at least 3 inches thick where the mortise holes are, as in most early beds? A smaller dimension may indicate that the post has been returned or that it is new.

3. Is the bed more than 76 inches long? Most early beds are no longer than this, so greater length may indicate that the side rails have been replaced or pieced out.

4. If there are Roman numerals cut into the rails and posts, is the writing (chiseling) style the same? A different style may indicate that some parts were made recently.

5. Is there dust in the mortises? This can be an indication of age, although some fakers have learned to "dirty up" the mortises.

6. Are there iron catches to hold the rails into the post or flat grooves cut into the rails to accommodate slats (rather than rope)? These are good indications that the bed was made no earlier than 1830—probably later.

7. Does the headboard or the footboard have any new saw cuts?

8. Do the posts, headboard, and footboard have the same paint history?

139

139. Daybed (1700–1820)

Is essentially a long chair with six or eight legs. Daybeds were made in the various chair styles. The backs are usually canted for comfort. Some early examples made before about 1750 have adjustable backs that are hinged with a dowel at the bottom and held by a chain at the top. The seats may be rush, splint, or upholstered.

Fig. 139: New England, 1700–1735.

Made in all regions, usually in hard woods.

Rare in country versions. Exp. to v. exp.

140, 141. Press Bed (1700–1830)

Has hinged side rails that fold upward, allowing the bed to be stored in a press (cupboard) or closet. The six-legged variety, hinged at the middle set of legs (fig. 140), is an earlier design than the type with four legs hinged at the head (fig. 141).

Beds similar to fig. 140 but with a simple, high canopy frame that extends toward the

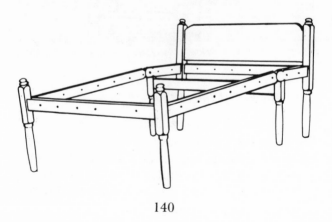

140

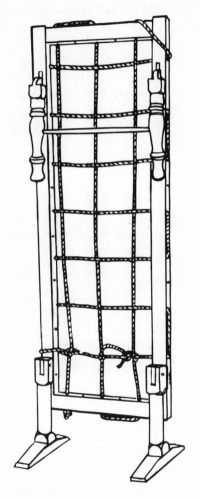

141

foot of the bed as far as the hinge are sometimes called slaw beds. Not intended to be
stored in a press, the rear of the bed folds up
into its own curtains draped over the canopy.

Fig. 140: New England, 1700–1760.

Fig. 141: Possibly New England, 1810–30.
Note the shoe feet at the head of the bed.

Made primarily in New England, usually in
maple and pine.

Not numerous. Mod. exp. to exp.

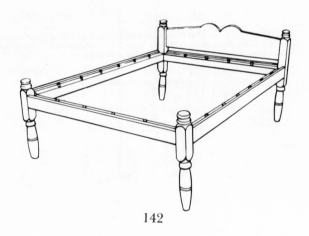

142

142. *Under-Eaves or Low-Post Bed (1700–1840)*

Has short posts and a low headboard no
more than about 3½ feet tall. The headboards
are usually straight, arched, or double arched

(fig. 142); later beds may have more elaborate scrolling, as in fig. 145.

As the name implies, these beds may have been used in the corners of attic rooms where the low roof limited the height of the posts.

Fig. 142: Possibly New England, 1740–1800. Made in all regions in hard and soft woods. Numerous. Mod. exp. to exp.

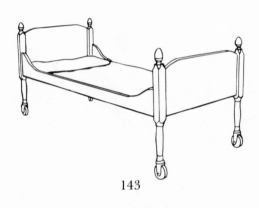

143

143. *Trundle Bed (1760–1840)*

Is a very low piece that usually has wheels, allowing it to be easily rolled under another bed for storage. The wheels may or may not swivel.

Trundle beds were most often made for children and were popular in the nineteenth century.

Fig. 143: Shaker community at Mount Lebanon, New York, nineteenth century.

Made in all regions in hard and soft woods. Fairly numerous. Mod. exp. to exp.

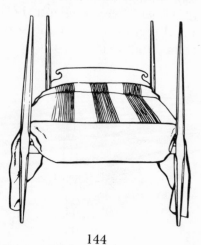

144

144. *Pencil-Post Bed* (1750–1840)

Has posts that are six- or eight-sided, fluted, or round. The posts may support a framework over which a full-length tester (canopy) can be draped.

Thin posts are taken as an indication of good style, which is why these beds are sometimes found with "improved" posts.

Fig. 144: New England, 1800–1830.

Made primarily in New England in hard or soft woods.

Fairly rare. Mod. exp. to v. exp.

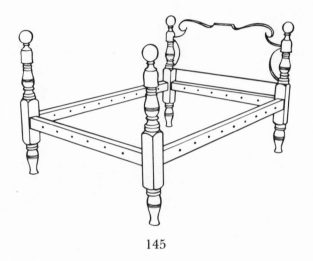

145

145. Cannonball Bed (1820–40)

Has heavy posts topped by large balls and an elaborately scrolled headboard. Cannonball beds sometimes have footboards.

Fig. 145: Possibly New England, 1820–40. Compare the shape of the headboard with the backboard on fig. 87.

Made in all regions, usually of maple and pine.

Fairly common. Inexp. to exp.

GLOSSARY
PICTURE INDEX
STYLE INDEX
FURTHER READING

GLOSSARY

Early furniture makers often used colorful but vague terms to describe the products in their advertisements and inventories. For example, cabriole legs are sometimes called "crookt feet," baluster-and-reel front stretchers are known as "turned frunts," and a comb-back Windsor chair might be a "highback'd chair." On the other hand, many of the early terms were specific and have survived almost unchanged, such as "secritary," "banester-backt chair," and "cornaic" (cornice).

Today, the terms used by collectors and dealers are generally more standardized. While in no way exhaustive, this glossary defines many of the terms you will hear in discussions about furniture and will read in auction advertisements, other antiques books, and antiques periodicals. The descriptive names for the various forms of furniture pictured in Chapters 6 through 13 are not usually defined here but are referred to by figure number. Terms in italics are defined under their own headings.

ABSENTEE, OR POCKET, BID: A bid left with an auctioneer prior to an auction by a person who cannot attend the actual auction. When a piece sells to an absentee bidder, it is said to have been sold "to the book."

ACORN FINIAL: A chair *Finial* resembling an inverted acorn that became a fairly standardized feature of certain Delaware Valley slat-back chairs. See, e.g., fig. 7.

ALL-ORIGINAL: Refers to a piece all of whose original parts are intact except, perhaps, for minor or early repairs.

APPLIED ARM: A heavy, separate piece of wood at the back of certain chairs, such as low-back Windsors. See, e.g., fig. 27.

APPLIED MOLDING: A separate strip of molding attached with brads, pins, or glue. Cf. *Run-in molding*.

APOTHECARY CHEST: See fig. 108.

APRON: Same as *Skirt*.

ARCHITECTURAL: Refers to a piece that was built into a room as part of its architecture, e.g., an architectural corner cupboard. Also refers to stylistic elements of a piece borrowed from architecture.

ARM SUPPORT OR STUMP: The vertical post that supports the arm of a chair.

ARROW-BACK CHAIR: See fig. 38.

AS IS: In auctioneers' lingo, often a euphemism for damaged.

BACKBOARDS: The boards attached to the back of a *Case piece.*

BACK POSTS: The rear uprights of a chair above the seat.

BAIL HANDLE: A semicircular brass or iron loop attached to posts and serving as a drawer pull. See, e.g., fig. Q, p. 101.

BALL FOOT: The more-or-less ball-shaped foot characteristic of William and Mary-style furniture. See, e.g., fig. 111.

BALL HANDHOLD: A ball-shaped chair *Handhold* that is the same diameter as the post on which it is turned.

BALL TURNING: Closely spaced, ball-shaped turnings on chair posts, table stretchers, etc.

BALUSTER: A squat or elongated turning that begins with a narrow neck and flares out to a rounded shape. See, e.g., the front stretcher of fig. 7.

BAMBOO TURNING: A turning that resembles bamboo, most characteristic of certain nineteenth-century Windsor chairs. See, e.g., fig. 31.

BANC-LIT: See fig. 42.

BANDY LEG: A squat, *Chippendale*-style *Cabriole leg.* See, e.g., fig. 112.

BANISTER-BACK CHAIR: See figs. 9–11.

BARREL BACK: Refers to a corner cupboard or a settle whose back is curved, thus resembling the staves of a barrel. See, e.g., fig. 41.

BASE MOLDING: The *Applied molding* around the base of a *Case piece.*

BATTEN: Same as *Cleat.*

BAT'S WING MOUNT OR BRASS: See figs. R and S, pp. 101 and 102.

BEADING: Narrow, half-round, *Run-in molding.* Sometimes used on country furniture to imitate *Cock-beading.*

BEDSIDE TABLE OR STAND: See figs. 82–84.

BIBLE BOX: See fig. 109.

BIRDCAGE: The four small vertical posts beneath the top of certain *Tip-and-turn tables.*

BIRDCAGE WINDSOR CHAIR: A chair resembling fig. 35 but with the second, fourth, and sixth spindles protruding to replace the butterfly medallion.

BLANKET BOX: A purist term for a *Chest* with no drawers.

BLANKET CHEST: Almost any *Chest.* To a purist, a *Chest over drawer or drawers.*

BLIND DOVETAIL: A dovetail whose leading edge is hidden because it stops short of penetrating the piece of wood to which it is attached.

BLIND NAILING: A method of nailing lap-joined boards so that the nails are hidden within the joint.

BLIND WEDGE: A wedge in the end of, for example, a Windsor chair leg that is hidden within the seat socket because the socket is not open.

BLOCK FRONT: Refers to certain case pieces, usually high style, whose fronts are shaped into three vertical blocks, the central block being recessed.

BLUNT ARROW FOOT: A type of foot most commonly found on certain Pennsylvania Windsor chairs. See, e.g., fig. 28.

BONNET TOP: A solid, double-arched top on certain tall, usually high-style *Queen Anne* and *Chippendale* case pieces such as the *Highboy* or the *Secretary*.

BOOTJACK FOOT: A foot resembling a bootjack formed by a triangular cutout in the bottom of the sides of certain simple case pieces. See, e.g., fig. 89.

BOSS: A type of early applied ornament that resembles an egg split in half.

BOSTON ROCKER: See fig. 40.

BOTTOM RAIL: The lower cross piece between the *Back posts* of certain chairs, such as the *Banister-back chair*. Cf. *Crest rail*.

BOW-BACK WINDSOR CHAIR: See figs. 30 and 31.

BOW FRONT: Refers to a *Case piece* whose front is convex.

BOX STRETCHERS: *Stretchers* arranged in a rectangle. See, e.g., fig. 110.

BRACED- OR BRACE-BACK: Refers to a *Continuous-arm Windsor chair, Fanback Windsor chair,* or *Bow-back Windsor chair* that has two extra bracing *Spindles* running from a *Tailpiece* to the bow or *Comb piece*. See, e.g., fig. 33.

BRACKET FOOT: A scrolled foot characteristic of *Queen Anne* and *Chippendale* furniture. See, e.g., figs. 101 and 104. Cf. *French foot*.

BRAD: A small finishing nail used to attach *Applied molding*.

BRAND: The name of the maker stamped or burned into a piece of furniture.

BREADBOARD ENDS: Transverse pieces of wood attached to the ends of a tabletop, edges of a door, etc., to keep them from warping and to hide the *End wood.* See, e.g., fig. 75.

BREWSTER CHAIR: A seventeenth-century chair with turned spindles in the back and below the front of the seat.

BUCKET BENCH: See fig. 134.

BUN FOOT: A flattened *Ball foot.*

BUTT HINGE: See fig. O, p. 98.

BUTT JOINT: The simplest wood *Joint* in which the flat edges of two boards butt against each other with no overlap. Also, a similar joint used where a tabletop leaf meets the central top. See fig. A, p. 79, and fig. 85, respectively.

BUTTERFLY HINGE: See fig. L, p. 96.

BUTTERFLY TABLE: See fig. 60.

BUTTON FOOT: A simplified *Pad foot* that resembles a button. See fig. 82.

CABINETMAKING: The making of the main structures of furniture by methods other than *Mortise-and-tenon joints,* e.g., by *Dovetail joints.*

CABRIOLE LEG: An essentially S-shaped leg characteristic of *Queen Anne* and *Chippendale* furniture. See, e.g., fig. 100.

CANDLE SLIDE: A small sliding platform built into a *Case piece* or a stand to support a candlestick.

CANNONBALL BED: See fig. 145.

CARCASE: The boxlike framework of a *Case piece* of furniture exclusive of any drawers, doors, applied molding, etc.

CARD TABLE: See fig. 75.

CARVER CHAIR: See fig. 1.

CASE PIECE: A piece of furniture whose main structure is boxlike, e.g., a chest of drawers.

CHAIR TABLE: See figs. 52 and 53.

CHAMFER: The beveled edge of a panel, drawer bottom, chair leg, etc.

CHASING: Engraved, as opposed to stamped, patterns on furniture brasses. Less commonly, a synonym for embossing.

CHEST: See figs. 88–90.

CHEST ON CHEST: See fig. 103.

CHEST OVER DRAWER OR DRAWERS: See figs. 91–93.

CHIP CARVING: Closely spaced, semicircular chips usually removed from the edge of a piece for decoration. See, e.g., fig. 109.

CHIPPENDALE: A period or style of furniture with distinctive characteristics. See pp. 109 and 110–11.

CLAW-AND-BALL FOOT: A foot carved in the shape of an animal claw clutching a ball. Characteristic of *Queen Anne* and *Chippendale* furniture; not usually found on country furniture.

CLEAT: A transverse board running under a tabletop, across the back of a door, etc.

CLINCH HINGE: Same as *Cotter-pin hinge.*

CLOSED CUPBOARD: A cupboard with doors. See, e.g., fig. 129. Cf. *Open cupboard.*

CLUB FOOT: A heavy *Pad foot.* See, e.g., fig. 14.

COCK-BEADING: Narrow, half-round, *Applied molding* around a drawer front or on the case around a drawer front.

COMB PIECE: The shaped *Crest rail* on a *Comb-back Windsor chair* or *Fanback Windsor chair*.

COMB-BACK WINDSOR CHAIR: See figs. 28 and 32.

CONSOLE TABLE: Same as *Half-round table*.

CONTINUOUS-ARM WINDSOR CHAIR: See fig. 33.

CORNER BLOCK: A carved block of wood at the intersection of the *Seat rails* and legs of *Slip seat* and upholstered chairs that adds structural strength.

CORNER CHAIR: Same as *Roundabout chair*.

CORNER CUPBOARD: See figs. 124 and 125.

CORNER POST: A square post at the corner of a *Case piece*.

CORNICE: The uppermost horizontal molding on a *Case piece,* such as a *Highboy*.

COTTER-PIN BRASS OR MOUNT: A drawer pull whose handle and backing plate are held in place by one or two cotter pins usually clinched back into the inside of the drawer front. See figs. P and Q, pp. 100 and 101.

COTTER-PIN HINGE: See fig. K, p. 95.

COURT CUPBOARD: A seventeenth-century form of cupboard with a closed top and an open base with a shelf.

COVE MOLDING: Concave *Cornice* molding. See, e.g., fig. 131.

CREST RAIL: The upper cross piece between the *Back posts* of certain chairs, such as the *Banister-back chair*. Cf. *Bottom rail*.

CROSS BASE: Same as X-base. See *X-base candlestand*.

CROSS STRETCHERS: Same as *X-stretchers*.

CUT DOWN: Refers to the legs of a chair, table, desk,

etc., that have been shortened. See, e.g., fig. 2. Cf. *Pieced out.*

DADO: A rectangular groove cut into a board to receive the end of another board. Sometimes used as a synonym for *Rabbet.*

DAYBED: See fig. 139.

DENTIL MOLDING: Molding that resembles widely spaced teeth.

DESK BOX: Same as *Writing box.*

DISH TOP: The round top of a table or stand that is dished out flat in the center, leaving a rounded, raised edge on the circumference. See, e.g., fig. 68.

DOCUMENT DRAWER: A tall, narrow drawer fitted into the interior of a desk.

DOTAGE: The signs of wear and age on the bottom of a foot.

DOUBLE-ARCH MOLDING: *Applied molding* that looks like two contiguous half-rounds, characteristic of *William and Mary* furniture. Usually considered later than *Single-arch molding.* See, e.g., fig. 97.

DOUBLE-BEARING OR -BRACED ARM: A chair arm that is set back from the front of the chair and whose support penetrates or is attached to the *Seat rung* and the first side *Rung.* See, e.g., fig. 22.

DOUGH BOX TABLE: See fig. 62.

DOVETAIL JOINT: A *Joint* formed from a triangular piece cut at the end of a board that fits into a triangular cutout in the end of another board. See, e.g., fig. D, p. 81.

DOWEL HINGE: A wooden hinge consisting of a dowel and the socket in which it pivots. Most commonly found on *Till* lids.

DOWER CHEST: See fig. 93.

DRAKE FOOT: Same as *Trifid foot.*

DRAWER SEPARATOR OR BLADE: The strip of wood that separates the front of one drawer from another in a *Case piece.*

DRESSER: Same as *Open cupboard.*

DRESSING TABLE: See fig. 87. Also used as a synonym for *Lowboy.*

DROP: A turned, pendantlike ornament. See, e.g., fig. 100.

DROP-LEAF TABLE: Any table with one or more hinged leaves that can be raised parallel to, and lowered perpendicular to, the floor.

DRY SINK: See figs. 135 and 136.

DUCKBILL ARM: On a *Rod-back Windsor chair,* an arm that meets the *Arm support* with no overhang, forming a point.

DUCK FOOT: Same as *Pad foot.*

DUST BOARD: A shelflike board that completely separates the drawers of a *Case piece.*

DUTCH CUPBOARD: See fig. 128.

DUTCH FOOT: Same as *Club foot.*

EAR: An extension of a chair's *Crest rail* or *Comb piece* beyond the *Back posts.* See, e.g., figs. 16 and 28.

EMPIRE FURNITURE: A redesigned *Sheraton*-style furniture. Made from about 1820 to 1840, it is basically characterized by bulkiness, *Reverse curves,*

dark or contrasting light and dark veneers, and
Mushroom knobs. The heavier forms have not es-
tablished themselves as desirable for the collector
of country furniture. However, lighter forms
such as figs. 87 and 116 are sometimes called
Empire and may be desirable. Some experts consider the *Hitchcock chair* to be Empire. Technically, this type of furniture is called American
Empire to distinguish it from French Empire
furniture.

ENDED OUT: Same as *Pieced out.*

END WOOD: The exposed wood cut across the grain
at the end of a board, as on a tabletop or desk
lid. End wood is often hidden by *Breadboard ends.*

ESCUTCHEON: A brass plate surrounding a keyhole.
Also used to describe the *Inlay* around a keyhole.

FAKE: A *Reproduction* made and/or sold to deceive
the buyer.

FALL-FRONT DESK: See figs. 118 and 119.

FANBACK WINDSOR CHAIR: See fig. 29.

FANCY CHAIR: Almost any paint-decorated Sheraton
chair, the premier example being the Hitchcock
chair. See figs. 20 and 21.

FARM TABLE: Same as *Work table.*

FEDERAL FURNITURE: According to Wallace Nutting,
refers to furniture made from 1776 to 1791; according to Dean A. Fales, from 1788 to 1820; according to Moreton Marsh, from 1780 to about
1830. In the antiques trade the term is used am-
biguously to describe furniture in the *Hepplewhite, Sheraton,* and *Empire* styles.

FIDDLE-BACK CHAIR: A chair that has what is essentially a Queen Anne *Splat* turned upside down. Compare fig. 12 with fig. 21.

FIELD BED: Same as *Tester bed.*

FIELDED PANEL: Same as *Raised panel.*

FIGURED: Refers to certain woods, such as tiger maple, that have a distinctive natural pattern in addition to the normal grain pattern.

FINGER HINGE: A wooden hinge resembling a squared-off *Dovetail joint,* most commonly used to attach the movable legs of a swing-leg table. See, e.g., fig. 74.

FINIAL: Any terminal, vertical, ornamental turning, such as at the top of the *Back posts* of a chair.

FISHTAIL BANISTER-BACK CHAIR: Same as *Staghorn banister-back chair.*

FLUTING: A series of half-round grooves carved out of the length of a leg, *Corner post,* etc. Cf. *Reeding.*

FOX OR FOXTAIL WEDGE: Same as *Wedge.*

FRENCH FOOT: Classically, a tapering *Bracket foot* that sweeps outward, characteristic of *Hepplewhite* furniture. Fig. 118 has a country variation of a French foot even though it is not outswept.

GALLERY: A rail or built-up ridge on the sides and back of the top of some desks, cupboards, stands, etc. See, e.g., fig. 86.

GATELEG TABLE: See fig. 56.

GEOMETRIC MOLDING: *Applied molding* arranged in various polygonal patterns. See, e.g., fig. 95.

GLAZED: Having panes of glass.

GRADUATED: Of increasing or decreasing vertical size. E.g., fig. 10 has graduated slats; fig. 73 has graduated drawers.

GRAIN PAINTING OR DECORATION: Paint applied to imitate the grain of certain woods.

GUDGEON: The socket in one half of a hinge into which the *Pintle* fits.

H HINGE: See fig. N, p. 97.

HL HINGE: See fig. N, p. 97.

H STRETCHERS: Stretchers arranged in the form of the letter H. Commonly refers to the stretcher arrangement on most Windsor chairs. Cf. *Medial stretcher; Box stretchers.*

HADLEY CARVING: Shallow carving in various organic shapes like that found on a *Hadley chest.* See, e.g., fig. 109.

HADLEY CHEST: A rare, early form of chest with carving similar to that of fig. 109, made in and around Hadley, Massachusetts.

HALF-ROUND TABLE: See fig. 67.

HALF-SPINDLE: Refers to certain nineteenth-century *Plank seat* chairs and settees whose *Spindles* extend from the seat only about halfway up the back. See, e.g., fig. 46.

HANDHOLD: The end of a chair arm or *Arm support* where the hand normally rests.

HARVEST TABLE: See fig. 85.

HEART-AND-CROWN BANISTER-BACK CHAIR: See fig. 9.

HEPPLEWHITE: A period or style of furniture with distinctive characteristics. See pp. 109 and 111.

HIGHBOY: See figs. 97–99.

HIGH CHEST: A purist term for a *Highboy*. Sometimes used as a synonym for *Tall chest*.

HITCHCOCK CHAIR: See fig. 20.

HOOP-BACK WINDSOR CHAIR: Same as *Sack-back Windsor chair*.

HOOPSKIRT ROCKER: See fig. 22.

HUTCH: A storage box built into a piece of furniture.

HUTCH TABLE: See fig. 59.

INLAY: Decorative pieces of wood or wax set flush into the surface of a board that contrasts in grain and/or color with that surface. In country furniture, sometimes imitated with paint.

IN THE ROUGH: Refers to a piece of furniture in need of repairs or restoration.

"JAM" CUPBOARD: Same as *"Jelly" cupboard*.

"JELLY" CUPBOARD: See fig. 131.

JOINERY: Construction by *Mortise-and-tenon joints*. Cf. *Cabinetmaking*.

JOINT: Any point at which two structural parts of a piece of furniture touch or are attached to each other.

KAS: See figs. 126 and 127.

KERF MARK: The mark left on a board by a saw blade.

KNEEHOLE DESK: A flat-top desk, usually with two tiers of several drawers flanking an opening for the user's knees. Sometimes there is a cupboard in the kneehole opening. An uncommon form in country furniture.

KNUCKLE HANDHOLD: A *Handhold* carved to resemble a person's knuckles. See, e.g., fig. 32.

KNUCKLE HINGE: Same as *Finger hinge.*

LADDER-BACK CHAIR: A type of Chippendale chair, such as fig. 17. Also, often used as a synonym for Slat-back chair.

LAP JOINT: See fig. H, p. 85.

LIBRARY TABLE: See figs. 54 and 55.

LIFT-TOP COMMODE: See fig. 137.

LIGHT: A small window. Fig. 128 might be called a "twelve-light cupboard."

LINEN PRESS: See fig. 130.

LIPPED OR LIP DRAWER: A drawer whose front is wide and tall enough to hide the drawer opening. See, e.g., fig. 104.

LOCKER: A small cupboard fitted into the interior of a desk.

LOOP-BACK WINDSOR CHAIR: Same as *Bow-back Windsor chair.*

LOWBOY: See fig. 100.

LOWER CASE: The bottom section of a two-part *Case piece.* The top section, of course, is the upper case.

LOW-POST BED: See fig. 142.

MAMMY BENCH: See fig. 47.

MARKET VALUE: The putative retail cash value of a piece if sold on the open market.

MARLBOROUGH FOOT: A square foot at the end of a

square Chippendale leg. Uncommon on country furniture.

MARRIAGE: The uniting of two different parts from two different pieces to form a new piece, which is essentially a fake. Frequently refers to a piece whose *Upper case* and *Lower case* come from two different sources.

MATCHSTICK MOLDING: Closely spaced, vertical bands of molding that resemble matchsticks. See, e.g., fig. 131.

MEDIAL STRETCHER: A stretcher that connects two side stretchers, usually at their centers. See, e.g., fig. 51. Cf. *H stretchers; Box stretchers.*

MIDMOLDING: The horizontal *Applied molding* at the point where an *Upper case* and a *Lower case* fit together, as in a *Highboy.*

MILK PAINT: A nineteenth-century furniture paint apparently based on skim milk, pigments, and various hardeners.

MITERED: Refers to boards, molding strips, etc., whose ends are usually cut at a 45-degree angle and form a 90-degree angle when butted against each other. The front feet and molding on fig. 104 are mitered.

MONKEY: A piece that has had parts added to or removed from it to "improve" it and enhance its value (i.e., it has been monkeyed with).

MORTISE: A rectangular hole cut in a table leg, chair post, etc., to accept a *Tenon.*

MORTISE-AND-TENON JOINT: See fig. F, p. 82.

MOUNT: A metal drawer pull.

MUNTINS: The strips of wood that separate and hold panes of glass, e.g., in a cupboard door.

MUSHROOM HANDHOLD: A flattened *Handhold* that is of greater diameter than the leg post on which it is turned or attached. See, e.g., fig. 3.

MUSHROOM KNOB: A wooden drawer pull that is wider than it is long. See, e.g., fig. 65.

OF THE PERIOD: Refers to a piece that is not only in a certain *Style* but was also made during the *Period* when that style was current.

OGEE BRACKET FOOT: An S-shaped *Bracket foot* characteristic of Chippendale furniture. Ogee is sometimes abbreviated O.G. See, e.g., fig. 127.

OGEE SCROLL: Scrolling with *Reverse curves*. See, e.g., fig. 121.

OPEN CUPBOARD: See figs. 121–23.

OPEN MORTISE: A *Mortise* that completely penetrates the wood into which it is cut, revealing the end of the *Tenon*. See, e.g., fig. 69, the middle crosspiece of which has two open mortises.

OXBOW: Usually refers to the front of a *Case piece* that has two outward curves flanking a central *Reverse curve;* the opposite of *Serpentine*. See, e.g., fig. 113.

PAD FOOT: A rounded, flattish foot on a *Cabriole leg* or *Straight cabriole leg*. See, e.g., fig. 70.

PANEL CONSTRUCTION: Made with *Rails* and *Stiles* enclosing panels.

PATINA: The thin layer of nicks, dents, age coloration, etc., that antique furniture acquires over the years. (Pronounced PA-tin-uh, not pa-TEEN-uh.)

PEG LEG: A *Spoke-shaved* or whittled leg inserted into a socket. See, e.g., fig. 68.

PEMBROKE TABLE: See fig. 76.

PENCIL-POST BED: See fig. 144.

PERIOD: An era of furniture making with a beginning and an end in which certain distinctive design features predominated. Cf. *Style.* See pp. 107–9.

PEWTER CUPBOARD: Same as *Open cupboard.*

PIECED OUT: Refers to the legs of a chair, table, etc., that have been restored to their original length. Cf. *Cut down.*

PIERCED: Cut out of the surrounding wood with a scroll saw, e.g., a pierced *Splat,* as in fig. 16. Also refers to the punched-out designs in the tin panels of a *Pie safe.*

PIE SAFE: See fig. 138.

PIGEONHOLE: An open storage compartment fitted into the interior of a desk.

PILGRIM-CENTURY FURNITURE: A term coined by Wallace Nutting that refers to seventeenth- and early eighteenth-century furniture before the William and Mary period. E.g., figs. 2 and 94 might be called Pilgrim-century furniture.

PIN: A polygonal dowel, usually of hard wood, that holds together a *Mortise-and-tenon joint.* See fig. F, p. 82.

PINTLE: The pin or shaft on one part of a hinge

that fits into a socket, or gudgeon, on the other part.

PLAIN SAWED: Refers to a board that has been sawed from a log without first quartering the log. Cf. *Quarter sawed.*

PLANK SEAT: A chair seat made from a single piece of wood.

POCKET BID: See *Absentee, or pocket, bid.*

POOL: A group of bidders, usually dealers, at an auction who attempt to restrain competition. See pp. 38–40.

PORRINGER TABLE: See fig. 70.

PRESS BED: See figs. 140 and 141.

PRESS CUPBOARD: A short, two-part seventeenth-century cupboard with a step-back, closed *Upper case* and a closed cupboard or drawers in the *Lower case.*

PRIMARY WOOD: In a *Case piece,* the wood from which the outer surfaces are largely constructed. Cf. *Secondary wood.*

PROVENANCE: The region where a piece originated, often determinable from distinctive stylistic features. Also, the history of successive owners of a piece.

QUARTER COLUMN: A reeded, fluted, molded, carved, etc., quarter-round *Corner post.*

QUARTER SAWED: Refers to a board, frequently oak, that has been sawed from a log that has first been sawed in quarters, which increases its resistance to warping. Cf. *Plain sawed.*

QUEEN ANNE: A period or style of furniture with distinctive characteristics. See pp. 109 and 110.

RABBET: See fig. B, p. 80.

RAIL: The horizontal piece of wood in *Panel construction,* as in a paneled cupboard door. Cf. *Stile.*

RAISED PANEL: A panel whose edges are chamfered, or beveled, raising the center of the panel away from its edges. See, e.g., fig. 127.

RAM'S HORN ARM SUPPORT: A swept-back, bent *Arm support.* See, e.g., fig. 31.

RANDOM-WIDTH BOARDS: A group of boards cut to nonuniform widths, such as in the *Backboards* of a cupboard. See, e.g., fig. 122.

RATCHET CANDLESTAND: See fig. 69.

RATTAIL HINGE: See fig. N, p. 97.

REBATE: Same as *Rabbet.*

REEDING: A series of raised half-rounds carved out of the length of a table leg, *Quarter column,* etc. Cf. *Fluting.*

REEL: A concave turning flanked by flanges.

REPRO OR REPRODUCTION: A piece made and/or sold as a faithful copy of an antique. Cf. *Fake.*

RESTORATION: Work done on a piece to restore its broken or missing parts, presumably to their original form.

RETAIL: Refers to a piece that was purchased by a collector as opposed to a dealer, with the implication that the price was higher than a dealer would have paid and that the piece is no longer on the market. Sometimes used pejoratively, as in, "It went retail."

REVERSE CURVE: A concave scroll on a *Skirt, Splat,* etc., that follows a convex scroll.

REVERSE SERPENTINE: Same as *Oxbow.*

RIGHT: Authentic and original in all respects. May refer to the whole or to the parts of a piece, as in, "Are those doors right?"

RING: A thick or thin circular turning. Also used as a synonym for *Pool.*

ROCKING SETTEE: See fig. 47.

ROD-BACK WINDSOR CHAIR: See figs. 35, 36, and 37.

ROPE BED: Any bed whose "springs" are formed from a network of ropes, as in fig. 141.

ROPE TURNING: Spiral *Reeding* that resembles a length of rope.

ROUNDABOUT CHAIR: See fig. 6.

RULE JOINT: On a drop-leaf table, a quarter-round mold on the edge of the central top that meets a quarter-round cutout along the edge of the leaf. See, e.g., fig. 73.

RUNG: A chair *Stretcher.*

RUN-IN MOLDING: Molding that is cut directly into the surface of a board. Cf. *Applied molding.*

RUNNER: A piece of wood inside a *Case piece* on which a drawer slides.

RUSH SEAT: A generic term for a chair or settee seat made of twisted, woven marsh grass or flag.

SACK-BACK WINDSOR CHAIR: See fig. 32.

SADDLE SEAT: The dished-out, body-conforming *Plank seat* of a Windsor chair that somewhat resembles the shape of a saddle with a pommel. See, e.g., fig. 32.

SALEM ROCKER: See fig. 39.

SAUSAGE TURNING: Turnings that resemble sausage links, most commonly found on certain rush- or splint-seat chair rungs. See, e.g., fig. 2.

SAWBUCK TABLE: See figs. 57 and 58.

SCHOOLMASTER'S DESK: See fig. 120.

SCHRANK: See fig. 127.

SCORE MARK: Same as *Scribe mark.*

SCRATCH CARVING: Shallow carving made with a pointed tool.

SCREW-POST CANDLESTAND: See fig. 68.

SCRIBE MARK: A shallow, narrow groove on a chair post, drawer, etc., used to mark the point of attachment of another part or the depth of a cut. On antique furniture, used instead of a pencil line. See, e.g., figs. D and F, pp. 81 and 82.

SCRUB OR SCRUBBED TOP: A tabletop, usually pine, that has been worn smooth and grayish white from scrubbing with soap and water.

SEAT RAILS: The horizontal pieces of wood linking the tops of the legs of upholstered and *Slip-seat* chairs.

SEAT RUNGS: The *Rungs* that form the framework around which a rush- and splint-seat is woven.

SECONDARY ARM: An arm below the upper arm of certain chairs. See, e.g., fig. 9.

SECONDARY WOOD: In a *Case piece,* the wood from which the interior parts are largely constructed.

SECRETARY OR SECRETARY DESK: See figs. 114–16.

SERPENTINE: Refers to the shape of certain tabletop edges, *Case piece* fronts, etc., that have a central outward curve flanked by *Reverse curves;* the opposite of *Oxbow,* or reverse serpentine. See, e.g., fig. 76.

SERVING TABLE: See figs. 65 and 66.

SETTEE: See figs. 45 and 46.

SETTLE BED: See fig. 42.

SHADOW MARK: The mark left under a tabletop from being in contact with the *Skirt* over the years.

SHADOW MOLDING: *Run-in molding* on the inner surface, as opposed to the edge, of a board. See, e.g., fig. 89.

SHAFT: Same as *Standard.*

SHERATON: A period or style of furniture with distinctive characteristics. See pp. 109 and 110.

SHERATON WINDSOR CHAIR: See fig. 35.

SHOE: A heavy, rounded extension at the bottom of a *Pad foot.* Also, a piece of wood attached to the rear *Seat rail* of certain Queen Anne and Chippendale chairs into which the *Splat* is mortised.

SHOE FOOT: A long, rail-like foot that often projects beyond the width of a piece. See, e.g., fig. 52.

SHOULDER: The rounded edge of a *Crest rail* that is usually flush with the *Back posts.*

SIDEBOARD: See figs. 65 and 66.

SIDE CHAIR: A chair without arms.

SINGLE-ARCH MOLDING: Applied half-round molding that is characteristic of *William and Mary* furniture. Usually considered earlier than *Double-arch molding.* See, e.g., fig. 91.

SIX-BOARD CHEST: Any chest made of six single boards. See, e.g., fig. 89.

SKINNED: Refers to a piece that has had its paint,

Patina, tool marks, and other signs of age sanded away or otherwise removed. A pejorative term used to describe a genuine antique that has been made to look like a bad reproduction.

SKIRT: The vertical boards that link the legs and are directly below the top of a table or at the base of a *Case piece.*

SLANT-FRONT DESK: Same as *Slant-lid desk.*

SLANT-LID DESK: See figs. 111–13.

SLAT ARM: A flattened chair arm. See, e.g., fig. 2.

SLIDES: On a desk, the pieces of wood that can be pulled out to support the lid.

SLIPPER CHAIR: A chair purposely made with a low seat, about 13 inches from the floor as opposed to the conventional 17 to 18 inches (i.e., you can put your slippers on more easily while sitting in it).

SLIPPER FOOT: A variation of a *Pad foot* that has a pointed toe, making it resemble a slipper.

SLIP SEAT: A rush or upholstered chair seat with its own frame that can be slipped out of the *Seat rails.*

SNAKE FOOT: A variation of a *Pad foot* that is elongated and vaguely resembles a snake's head. Fig. 81 has a type of snake foot.

SNIPE HINGE: Same as *Cotter-pin hinge.*

SPADE FOOT: A square, tapered foot at the end of a square, tapered leg or *Spider leg,* characteristic of *Hepplewhite* furniture. See, e.g., fig. 106.

SPANISH FOOT: A foot with carved, outswept, scrolled toes, characteristic of *William and Mary* furniture. See, e.g., fig. 12.

SPIDER LEG: An arched, often tapered square leg. See, e.g., fig. 78.

SPINDLES: The round, turned, or flattened rods that are socketed into and rise from the seat of certain chairs, most notably Windsors. (Note: A Windsor chair is often referred to by the number of spindles in its back, regardless of how many other spindles the chair may have; thus fig. 28 might be called "a nine-spindle comb-back Windsor chair.")

SPLAT: A broad, vertical piece of wood forming the back of certain chairs. See, e.g., figs. 12, 16, 19, and 21.

SPLAY: Refers to chair or table legs that angle forward, sideways, or both from their uppermost point of attachment. See, e.g., figs. 30 and 62.

SPLINE JOINT: See fig. H, p. 85.

SPLINT SEAT: A seat made of thin, interwoven strips of hickory, basswood, or other wood.

SPOKE SHAVED: Whittled to a cylindrical shape with a type of drawknife, as opposed to being turned on a lathe.

SPOKE STRETCHER: A rare form of *Stretcher* found on certain New England *Bamboo-turned* Windsor chairs in which the front legs are connected to each other by a backward bowed piece of steam-bent oak from which two straight stretchers radiate, like spokes, to either rear leg.

SPOON BACK: Generally refers to a Queen Anne chair whose back more or less conforms to the curvature of the human spine (i.e., it is shaped like a spoon in profile). See, e.g., fig. 12.

STAGHORN BANISTER-BACK CHAIR: See fig. b, p. 136.

STANDARD: The central shaft of a *Tripod table or stand.*

STAPLE HINGE: Same as *Cotter-pin hinge.*

STEP-BACK CUPBOARD: See fig. 129.

STEP-DOWN WINDSOR CHAIR: See fig. 36.

STICK-BACK WINDSOR CHAIR: Same as *Rod-back Windsor chair.*

STILE: The vertical piece of wood in *Panel construction,* as in a paneled cupboard door. Cf. *Rail.*

STILE FOOT: A foot formed by the extension of the corner stiles of certain case pieces. See, e.g., fig. 88.

STOP CHAMFERING, FLUTING, OR REEDING: *Chamfering, Fluting,* or *Reeding* with a visible beginning and ending point. The corners of fig. 131 are stop chamfered.

STRAIGHT CABRIOLE LEG: A cabriole leg without an S curve. See, e.g., fig. 70.

STRAPWORK: The piercing and carving of a chair *Splat* that resembles interlacing straps.

STRETCHER: A piece of wood that links and braces the legs of a chair, table, etc. A stretcher may also link other stretchers. Cf. *Box stretchers; H stretchers; Medial stretcher; Rung.*

STRINGING: Narrow lines of *Inlay.* Sometimes imitated on country furniture with paint. See, e.g., fig. 65.

STYLE: All the design features of a piece that are associated with a certain *Period* of furniture making; e.g., the base of fig. 12 is in the William and Mary style, the back in the Queen Anne style.

Sometimes used to describe a piece that is not *Of the period,* e.g., a "Chippendale-style chest of drawers" might have been made in 1952. Cf. *Period.* See pp. 109–16 and 377–78.

SUBTOP: In a *Case piece,* a secondary top below, and hidden by, the main top.

SUNFLOWER CHEST: A misnomer for a type of rare seventeenth- and early eighteenth-century Connecticut *Chest over drawers* with three shallowly carved oak panels representing such organic forms as tulips, roses, and thistles.

SURVIVAL: Not *Of the period,* with the implication of a certain design decadence. A frequently used term; however, is it not more precise to say, "That is a late eighteenth-century trestle table" than "That is a survival trestle table"?

SWING-LEG TABLE: See figs. 73 and 74.

TAILPIECE: The extension at the back of the seat of a *Brace-back* Windsor chair that supports the two extra *Spindles.* See, e.g., fig. 33.

TALL CHEST: See, e.g., fig. 104.

TAMBOUR DESK: See fig. 117.

TAVERN TABLE: See figs. 50 and 51.

TEA TABLE: See figs. 70–72. Sometimes used as a synonym for *Tip-and-turn table.*

TEARDROP BRASS OR MOUNT: See fig. P, p. 100.

TENON: A tonguelike projection cut at the end or edge of a board that fits into a *Mortise* in another board.

TESTER BED: A bed with a wooden framework to support a fabric canopy, or tester.

THUMB-BACK CHAIR: See fig. 37.

THUMB OR THUMBNAIL MOLDING: *Run-in molding* on the edge of a board that in cross section resembles the outline of the end of an upside-down thumb. See, e.g., fig. 137.

TILL: A storage compartment with a *Dowel-hinged* lid built into many chests at one or both ends just below the lift top.

TIP-AND-TURN TABLE: A *Tripod table* whose top can both rotate and tip vertically.

TOENAILING: Nailing at an angle through the *Skirt* of a table into the top.

TONGUE-AND-GROOVE JOINT: See fig. H, p. 85. Also, a similar joint used where a tabletop leaf meets the central top. See, e.g., fig. 56.

TOP RAIL: Same as *Crest rail.*

TORUS MOLDING: Convex *Cornice* molding. See, e.g., fig. 97.

TO THE BOOK: See *Absentee, or pocket, bid.*

TRANSITIONAL: A much used and abused term that usually refers to a chair that combines stylistic elements from two contiguous furniture periods, thus supposedly showing a transition between them. See pp. 114–15.

TRAY-TOP TABLE: See fig. 71.

TRESTLE TABLE: See figs. 48 and 49.

TRIFID FOOT: A foot with three toes at the end of a *Cabriole leg.* See, e.g., fig. 72.

TRIPOD TABLE OR STAND: See figs. 77–81.

TRUNDLE BED: See fig. 143.

TRUNNEL: Same as *Pin.*

TURN BUTTON: A small wooden block that pivots,

usually on a screw, and is used to hold a cup-board door closed. See, e.g., fig. 132.

TURNED: Literally, shaped on a lathe; however, frequently used as a synonym for ornamentally turned.

UNDERBIDDER: The person who makes the second highest bid at an auction (i.e., the runner-up).

UNDER-EAVES BED: See fig. 142.

UPPER CASE: The upper section of a two-part *Case piece*. The bottom section, of course, is the lower case.

URN FINIAL: An urn-shaped *Finial*.

VALANCE: A stylized, scrolled representation of drapery resembling the top of an upside-down heart, most commonly found on the *Skirts* of certain Hepplewhite pieces. See, e.g., fig. 118.

VASE TURNING: Same as *Baluster*.

VENEER: A glued-on, relatively thin layer of wood used for its beautiful or contrasting grain, frequently imitated on country furniture with paint.

WAGON SEAT: See fig. 44.

WAINSCOT: Technically, *Panel construction* in oak. Often used as a synonym for panel construction in any wood on a chest, chair, settee, etc.

WASHSTAND: See fig. 86.

WATER BENCH: See fig. 134.

WEDGE JOINT: See figs. I and J, p. 88.

WELSH DRESSER: See fig. 123.

WILLIAM AND MARY: A period or style of furniture with distinctive characteristics. See pp. 109 and 110.

WILLOW BRASS OR MOUNT: See fig. T, p. 102.

WINDSOR: Refers to any piece with style character-istics associated with the *Windsor chair*, e.g., a table with *Splayed* legs turned like fig. 30 would be called a Windsor table.

WINDSOR CHAIR: Generally, any chair with *Spindles* and legs socketed into a *Plank seat*. See, e.g., figs. 26–35.

WORK TABLE: See figs. 63 and 64.

WRITING-ARM WINDSOR CHAIR: See figs. 34 and 35.

WRITING BOX: See fig. 109.

X-BASE CANDLESTAND: See fig. 61.

X-STRETCHERS: Diagonal *Stretchers* forming an X.

YOKE-BACK BANISTER-BACK CHAIR: See fig. a, p. 136.

PICTURE INDEX

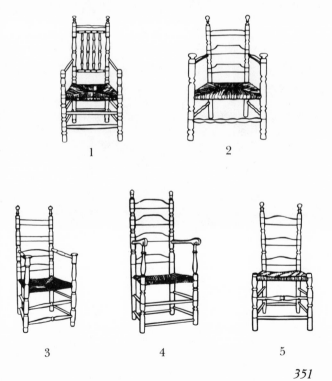

1

2

3

4

5

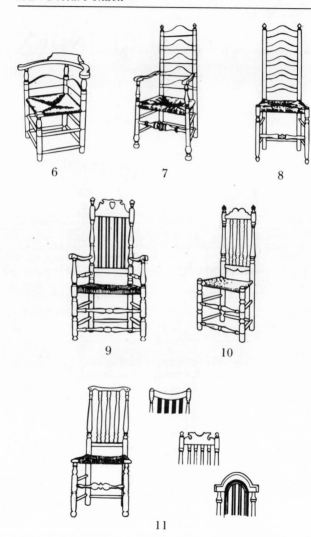

6

7

8

9

10

11

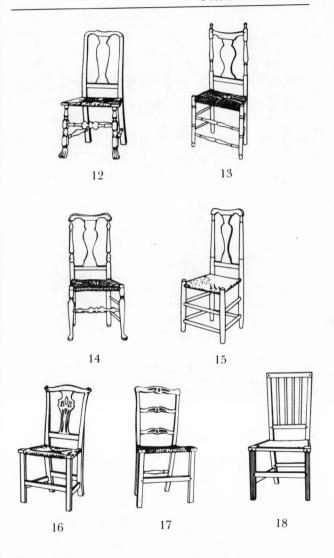

12   13

14   15

16   17   18

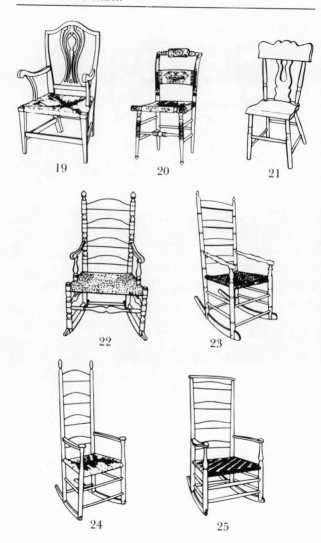

19   20   21

22   23

24   25

26

27

28

29

30

31

32

33

34

35

36

37

38

39

40

41

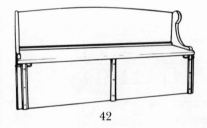

42

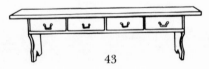

43

44

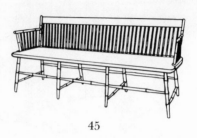

45

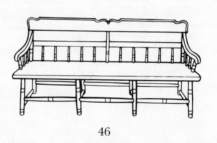

46

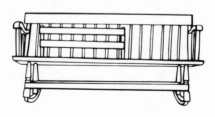

47

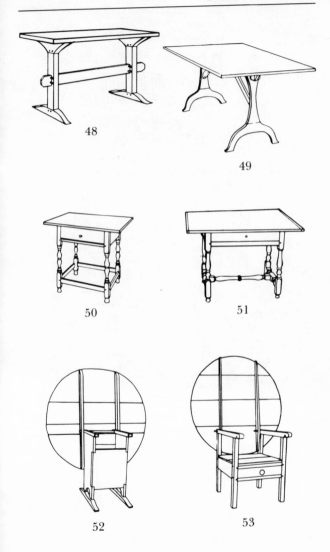

48

49

50

51

52

53

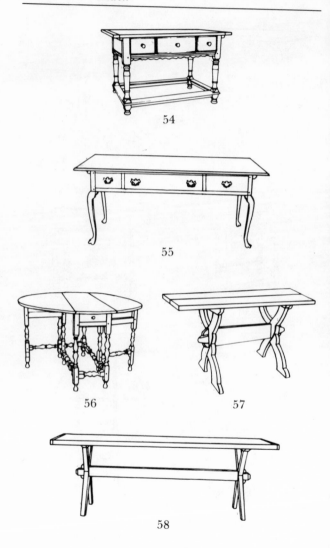

54

55

56

57

58

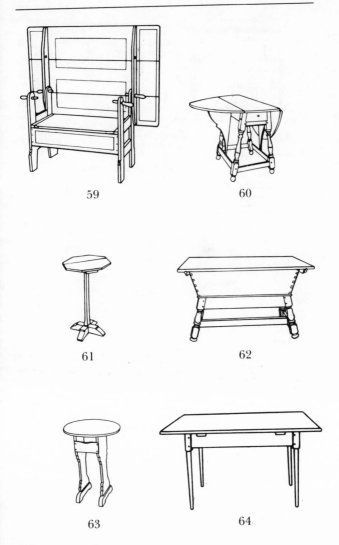

59

60

61

62

63

64

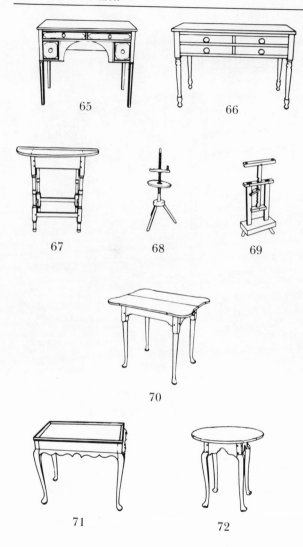

65

66

67

68

69

70

71

72

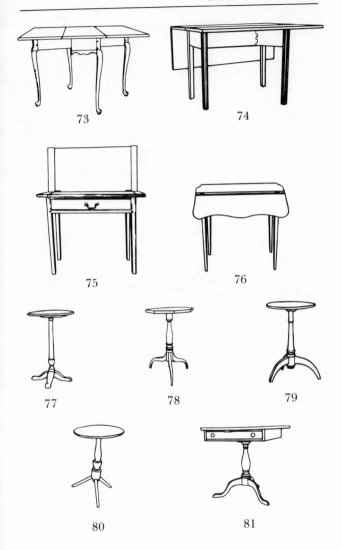

73

74

75

76

77

78

79

80

81

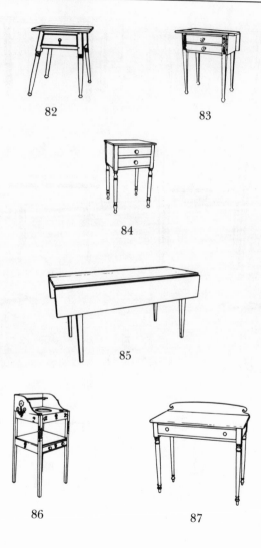

82

83

84

85

86

87

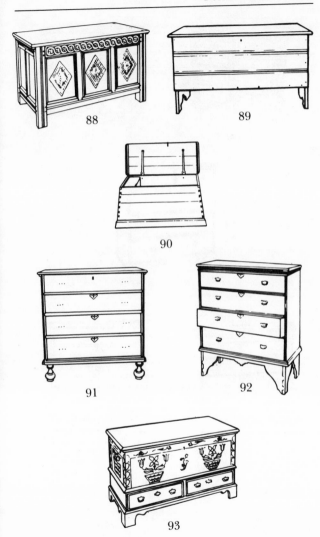

88

89

90

91

92

93

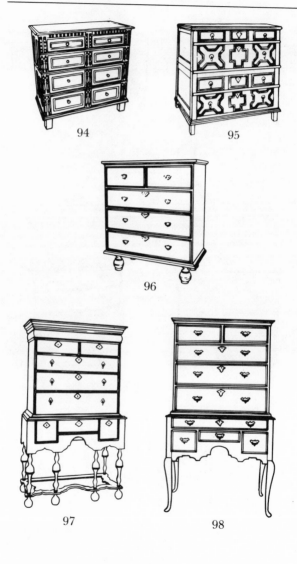

94

95

96

97

98

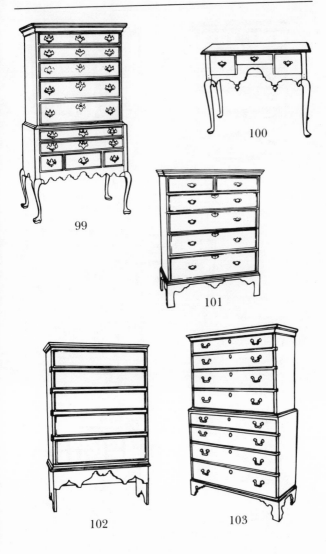

99

100

101

102

103

104

105

106

107

108

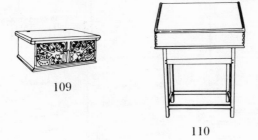

109

110

111

112   113

114

115

116

117

118

119

120

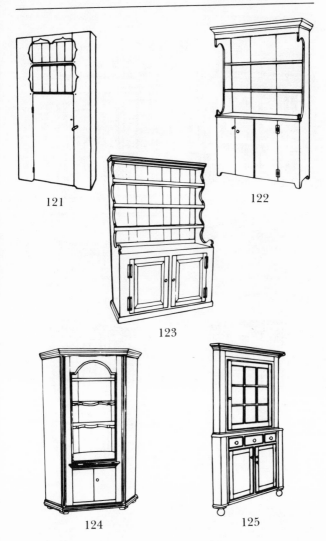

121

122

123

124

125

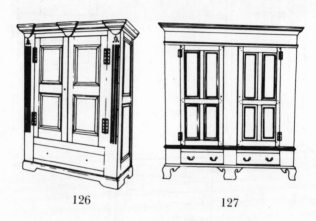

126

127

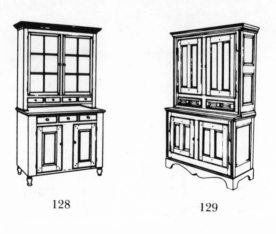

128

129

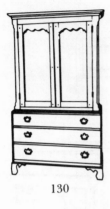

130

131

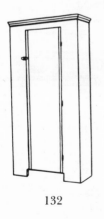

132

133

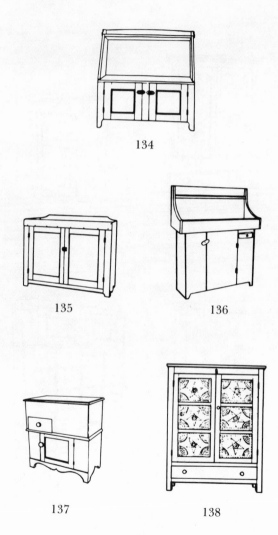

134

135

136

137

138

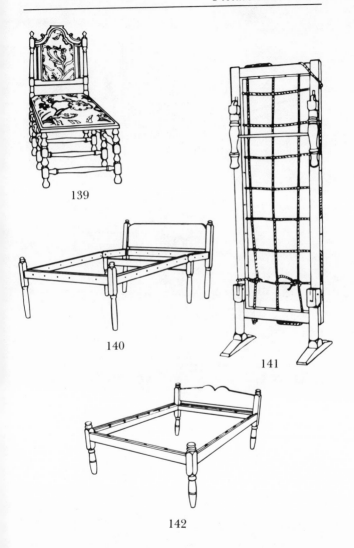

139

140

141

142

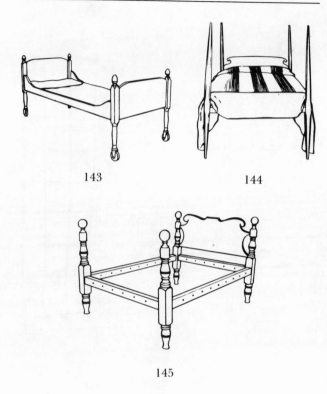

143

144

145

STYLE INDEX

Categorizing country furniture by style is sometimes about as fruitful as teaching a cat to bark. Nevertheless, many of the pieces illustrated in this book can be placed in a major style niche, and they are listed here by figure number.

Among other things, this index should lead you to appropriate illustrations in this book when you are reading unillustrated advertisements for furniture. Thus, for example, if you were looking for an illustration of a Chippendale chest of drawers, you would have only to look here—first under the main heading, Chippendale, then, below it, Chests and Chests of Drawers—to locate several examples.

For more information on the styles of country furniture, please see Chapter 4.

FURTHER READING

De Jonge, Eric, ed. *Country Things*. Princeton, N.J.:
The Pyne Press, 1973.
> *An atrociously printed, but occasionally intriguing,
> conglomeration of articles from past issues of The
> Magazine,* Antiques.
Fales, Dean A., Jr. *American Painted Furniture
1660–1880*. New York: E. P. Dutton, 1972.
> *A glossy but not too coffee-table-ish book, well worth
> having for the advanced collector and likely to be the
> last word on the subject for many years. Illustrated
> with color photographs.*
Hammond, Dorothy. *Pictorial Price Guide to Ameri-
can Antiques and Objects Made for the American Mar-
ket*. New York: E. P. Dutton, 1977.
> *I am not convinced of the value of price guides, but
> this one, with its more than 5,000 photographs, is
> probably the best of its kind. Still, it suffers from the
> typical limitations: not enough information, too
> much "junk," and dollar figures that have little
> meaning, as far as I have been able to determine.*
———. *Price Guide to Country Antiques and American
Primitives*. New York: Funk and Wagnalls, 1975.
> *The only price guide that deals exclusively with
> country things.*
Hummel, Charles F. *With Hammer in Hand: The Do-*

miny Craftsmen of East Hampton, New York. Charlottesville: The University Press of Virginia, 1968.

> *A book on the great country furniture-making family from Long Island. For the advanced collector.*

Kane, Patricia E. *300 Years of American Seating Furniture: Chairs and Beds from the Mabel Brady Garvan and Other Collections at Yale University.* Boston: Little, Brown (a New York Graphic Society Book), 1976.

> *A superb book for the advanced collector who craves solid information, with more than 300 remarkably clear photographs, some in color; but note that about forty of the pieces illustrated are nineteenth- and twentieth-century factory products, some modernistic.*

Kettell, Russell Hawes. *The Pine Furniture of Early New England.* New York: Dover Publications, 1949.

> *A classic book on the styles of New England country furniture made in pine, with 200 photographs and 55 measured line drawings. Highly recommended.*

Kirk, John T. *Early American Furniture.* New York: Alfred A. Knopf, 1970.

————. *The Impecunious Collector's Guide to American Antiques.* New York: Alfred A. Knopf, 1975.
> *Two extraordinary, well-illustrated books by the greatest contemporary writer on American antiques. Kirk has the remarkable ability to be simultaneously passionate and objective about furniture. The second book listed is a must for all collectors of country furniture.*

Kovel, Ralph M. and Terry H. *American Country*

Furniture, 1780–1875. New York: Crown Publishers, 1965.

A hodge-podge of illustrations of pieces of country furniture, some of which would have been better off left to rest in peace. Nevertheless, it is a useful book if you can distinguish the good from the bad. Some dates and information on provenance are seriously in error. Recommended.

Marsh, Moreton. *The Easy Expert in Collecting and Restoring American Antiques*. Philadelphia: J. B. Lippincott, 1959.

A minor classic, especially in the area of proper do-it-yourself restoration—knowledge that, even if not put into practice, is very useful in spotting restorations. Closeup photos of furniture parts. Highly recommended.

Meader, Robert F. W. *Illustrated Guide to Shaker Furniture*. New York: Dover Publications, 1972.

An excellent, concise, and readable book for those who want to know more about the construction and styles of Shaker furniture but not about the Shaker religion. A bonus feature is a reprint of a complete Shaker furniture catalog. Has 235 high-quality black-and-white photographs. Highly recommended.

Nutting, Wallace. *Furniture Treasury*. Vols. 1 and 2 in one [volume]. New York: Macmillan Publishing Company, 1928 (and later printings).

Illustrated with 5,000 photographs, this is the great pioneering work on furniture styles, including many country pieces. The text is sparse, informative, opinionated, and occasionally outdated. A must for any serious collector.

———. *Furniture Treasury.* Vol. 3. New York: Macmillan Publishing Company, 1933 (and later printings).

> *The companion volume to the previous listing, it is illustrated with line drawings, contains fascinating accounts of collecting in the early twentieth century, corrects some of the errors in vols. 1 and 2, and much more. Recommended.*

Ormsbee, Thomas H. *Field Guide to Early American Furniture.* New York: Bonanza Books, 1951.

> *Deals almost exclusively with high-style furniture. Very broad in scope; illustrated with line drawings. Recommended as an introduction to high-style furniture.*

Parsons, Charles S. *The Dunlaps and Their Furniture.* Manchester, New Hampshire: The Currier Gallery of Art, 1970.

> *An overview of the great country furniture-making family from New Hampshire. For the advanced collector.*

Sack, Albert. *Fine Points of Furniture: Early American.* New York: Crown Publishers, 1950.

> *A classic that takes the "good, better, best" approach to furniture design, most of it high style. It is good to own because of its 800 photographs and aesthetic comparisons of various pieces, but it generally takes a deprecatory view of country furniture. Some of Sack's dating and information on provenance is incorrect. Recommended.*

Schwartz, Marvin D. *American Furniture of the Colonial Period.* New York: The Metropolitan Museum of Art, 1976.

A solid introduction to high-style furniture through the Chippendale period, including some high-style country pieces. It is especially valuable for its information on the dimensions of, and wood used in, various pieces. Has color and black-and-white photographs.

Shea, John G. *Antique Country Furniture of North America.* New York: Van Nostrand Reinhold Company, 1975.

Valuable primarily because of its photographs of Canadian furniture. Has measured line drawings.

United States Department of Agriculture, Forest Service. *Wood: Colors and Kinds* (Agriculture Handbook 101). Washington, D.C.: U.S. Government Printing Office, 1956.

An excellent, inexpensive booklet on identifying wood types, with sixteen pages of color photographs on the end-, edge-, and flat-grains of thirty-two different American woods. Highly recommended.

Watson, Aldren A. *Country Furniture.* New York: Thomas Y. Crowell, 1974.

The best book about early woodworking methods and the construction of country furniture. Illustrated with the author's own explicit and beautiful halftone drawings. Highly recommended.

Williams, H. Lionel. *Country Furniture of Early America.* New York: A. S. Barnes, 1963.

Useful but not indispensable.